running with the bulls

running with the bulls

Luc Longley's championship season at Chicago.
WITH CHRIS APPLEBY

IRONBARK
Pan Macmillan Australia

Pictures courtesy of Bill Smith

First published 1996 in Ironbark by Pan Macmillan Australia Pty Limited
St Martins Tower, 31 Market Street, Sydney

Copyright © Luc Longley 1996

All rights reserved. No part of this book may be reproduced or transmitted in any form or by
any means, electronic or mechanical, including photocopying, recording or by any information
storage and retrieval system, without prior permission in writing from the publisher.

National Library of Australia
Cataloguing-in-Publication data:

Longley, Lucien James, 1969–
Running with the Bulls: Luc Longley's championship season at Chicago.

ISBN 0 330 35885 5.

1. Longley, Lucien James, 1969–. 2. Chicago Bulls (Basketball team). 3. Basketball players–
Australia–Biography. 4. Basketball players–United States–Biography. 5. Basketball–Illinois–
Chicago. I. Title.

796.32364092

Designed by Big Cat Design
Printed in Australia by McPherson's Printing Group

contents

	Foreword—by Phil Jackson	vii
	Prologue—scaling the summit	xi
1	JUST A BAD SITUATION	1
2	FINALLY, A BASKETBALL LIFELINE	7
3	BULLS MYSTIQUE, WHAT'S THAT?	11
4	INFLATED	15
5	A MENACE? NO WAY, NOT MY DENNIS	23
6	OUR ZEN MASTER	39
7	ELVIS IS IN THE BUILDING	51
8	THE BANK'S OPEN	63
9	ON THE ROAD WITH THE BEATLES	69
10	CLASS ACT	81
11	THE MARATHON BEGINS	85
12	BREAKING THE TEDIUM	101
13	POSTING UP IN THE POST SEASON vs Miami vs New York vs Orlando	107
14	THE BIG DANCE vs Seattle	119
15	THE RING IS THE THING, TIME TO PARTY	131
16	INJURY TIMEOUT	137
17	ESCAPING THE SOUL PIRATES	143
	Postscript—by Chris Appleby	146

All Luc Longley's proceeds from the sale of this book will go to the Longley Foundation to be used for the benefit of underprivileged children.

foreword

by Phil Jackson

*I*n July of 1990, general manager Jerry Krause and I went to Seattle to see the Goodwill Games. In the draft of that year we had selected Toni Kukoc as the 29th pick and wanted to see him play and get to know him. Jerry and I went to all the games that week and watched the young talent of the world play basketball. That was the first time I watched Luc Longley play basketball. As usual, Luc wasn't dominating in the post as a scorer, but he passed and shot the ball quite well and showed good athletic talent. I was intrigued by this young centre.

Luc went as a lottery pick the next year to Minnesota, 20 picks ahead of the Bulls, but we continued to watch his progress as a player in the NBA. It wasn't easy for a young player to fit in with a team finding its identity. In February of 1994, we were able to get Luc to the Bulls by trading our young centre Stacey King for him. If I recall my first meeting with Luc, I asked if he pronounced his name 'Luke' or 'Luck'. In his direct manner, Luc boldly stated that it was Luke. I told him he should go by LUCK now, because he was in luck by becoming a Bull. So it has been.

The luck of getting Luc was a two-way street, as we found this massive, bull-like redhead to be just the kind of player that would be a match for our system of play and the make-up of the Bulls. Luc has endeared himself to our team and Chicago with his honest, open style and his friendly demeanour, while maintaining his space on the court with determined play.

It wasn't by chance that we chose Luc. Our organisation watched many tapes of him playing basketball and they showed Luc to be a player of promise. When it came down to a decision to trade for Luc, I told Jerry Krause I saw him as an unselfish team player who would anchor the post in our sideline triangle offence and be a stopper at the defensive end where he was fearless. Luc wasn't known for his shot-blocking, even though he could block shots, but more importantly, he could plug the holes on defence. Those early predictions have proven to be right.

It has not been an easy road for Luc here in Chicago. He started out with the relief of a freed prisoner in March of 1994 as he got the chance to start due to injuries. Later during the play-offs, Bill Cartwright, our co-captain, returned to the starting line-up as we made our play-off run. Luc had shown promise and we held our hope he could shoulder the load for the future when Cartwright retired that Spring. But in the pre-season of the next year, Luc turned his ankle and suffered a stress fracture, which wasn't discovered until three weeks later. Luc missed almost half a season and never returned to the starting line-up in the 1994–95 season until the play-offs.

Playing without a power forward during that season, our centre crew had big problems rebounding and plugging the lane. The return of Michael Jordan that year didn't make it any easier for Luc either, as MJ chose to test Luc on many occasions. The season ended with a loss to Orlando Magic in which Luc had a critical shot blocked in the final minute of a disappointing game. We still believed Luc could be a vital part of a championship team and we turned to the 1995–96 season with hopes of regaining our status in the NBA.

In September, just before training camp began, we made a trade for Dennis Rodman. This acquisition gave us the rebounding edge we wanted, and it freed up Luc from the worry of protecting the lane, rebounding and defending his own man all in the same sequence of action. The teamwork of Luc and Dennis was fun to watch as they took turns defending post-up scorers by using either size and weight, or speed and savvy. Dennis was our designated bounder (inbounder) which enabled Luc to run the court on offence and anchor our sideline triangle. That aside, Luc's ability to befriend people allowed Dennis Rodman, an enigma at San Antonio, to become a teammate on and off the court with the Bulls.

Our 1995–96 season was a marathon of eight pre-season games, 82 regular season games and a total of 15 play-off wins to garner the championship. In those eight months, as we struggled together, there were moments of elation and dejection. That is the natural course of events. This particular year had all those emotions, but was more positive than I've ever experienced, and I say that not just because we won so many games. It was because of the people we had on the team. They were the oldest team in the league, and also the most diverse with four members born in foreign countries, which made this group international in its make-up. It also made this team a tolerant group as they weathered possible distractions, while keeping their course in a determined way.

On a two-week road trip west, Luc tore his knee in an unusual way making an offensive move. It was within a week of his wife giving birth to their second daughter. Luc went home to have his knee scoped and was home just in time for the birth of his child as if divinely guided. We won our next game without Luc, but then suffered our only back-to-back losses in the regular season. But unlike the previous year, Luc was back within the month and we continued on through our record-setting year. All things worked together for the Bulls in 1995–96 and we acknowledged that as we gratefully gave credit to each other and good fortune. My good fortune was to work with an exceptional group of men, of which Luc was a key member.

This book is an enjoyable view of the Bulls as they romped through the 'greatest season ever'. The historic 1995–96 NBA season was an effort by men like Luc, who loved the camaraderie of teammates and the challenge of competition. Luc has the gift of an analytical mind (which sometimes works against him on the basketball court), that will guide you through this season. Along with some pictorial help, Luc gives you an idea of what was created by this team—a community of men that worked together to enhance each other's strengths and hide individual weaknesses.

They did that by being honest with each other and committing to the group's common goal and it wasn't just to win the NBA championship—all players want that. What the Bulls did was learn how to enjoy the process of teamwork. That process is a daily focus of being the best by working together the best whether it be in practice or in a game. If Luc can recapture the essence of that process, you will have the inside story. ○

prologue
scaling the summit

The final buzzer for the season sounded and all the guys burst out to centre court and jumped on Michael. I found myself hanging back, almost like a spectator, watching and absorbing. When I thought about winning an NBA championship, I'd always expected I was going to want to cash in on all the hard work and go nuts. But it was a complete vacuum. Suddenly all the drive, everything that had gone in to the year was sucked out of me by this one accomplishment.

A minute later, the boys jumped on me, but really, I wanted to run into the locker room and just scream, release it all right there. I had my family in the stands, and for me it was more a proud moment than an adrenalin rush. It sort of hits you in the back of the head and you say, 'Okay, you can pat yourself on the back now'.

The championship was all about proving to myself that I was the real deal. To demonstrate my worth. I didn't think statistics showed it and I didn't think people understood what I'd done on this team, what my NBA career had been or how hard I'd worked. I felt to get it done would prove to me what I was capable of. Not that I ever doubted it, but it's nice to have that tangible evidence.

It's been quite a ride. The journey is the reward.

chapter 1

just a bad situation

Before being drafted seventh by the Wolves in 1991, I had purposely told the media I wasn't concerned where I ended up. I always thought I'd play at Denver, but that year the Nuggets took Georgetown centre Dikembe Mutombo at No.4 overall. I was the second centre taken. I was asked by the Minnesota media upon being drafted if I had even been ice fishing. In weather that got to 20 below, coupled with 30 inches of snow, I was about to find out what they were talking about.

From day one the Wolves organisation was all backwards. Then-general manager Bob Stein had little idea of the basketball business. He was a football agent and get this, the husband of one of the daughters of one of the owners. He'd done deals and contracts for his clients in the past, but he wasn't up to speed on handling employees.

Bob's a nice guy, but I think he had paid other players too much and had to play the tough guy with me. I wasn't asking for anything more than my scaled salary structure. I was asking for right on the mean line for a seventh pick, he wanted to pay me about a No.11. His argument was, we had two other centres (Felton Spencer and Randy Breuer) and I hadn't proven myself.

I missed all of training camp and several games, which really hurt me and the team. But I had support from the players when I arrived, they felt it was important for all players to stand up to management when needed and this was one of those cases. So it was a bad start from the point of view of my basketball career.

LUC LONGLEY

You should never finger roll over Dikembe Mutombo.

As an expansion team entering the league in 1989, obviously both the team and the organisation weren't very good. And the other thing that got me really down in the first year or two was the nature of the NBA and the professionalism of the league.

Impressionable as I was, I quickly ascertained guys were in this league to make money to support families. Example: On a fast-break three-on-one, three-on-two situation, they were going to the hole to score because it meant money. Passing was something you did on the freeway to the game. Another five points on your scoring average could mean another $1 million a season. To a team that's already losing, there tends to be a rule of 'Get out of it what you can, look good and hopefully get a big contract or get traded.'

That whole aspect of team spirit and sense of unity wasn't there.

I was used to college and Australian teams which were tight and you'd have a drink after the game. NBA players are mercenaries and you go your different ways after games. Because the turnover of personnel is so fast, you don't get to make the same friendships, there's not the same bond within the team or camaraderie with that selfish play on the court. I had good friends in Scott Brooks, Sam Mitchell and Thurl Bailey, these were guys I got to like and then they'd get traded. Then when I found some guys around the team that I liked, like Christian, I got traded.

The other destabilising factor was the bloated salaries. Players made so much more than the coach. Jimmy Rodgers, who had been the coach of the Boston Celtics (now an assistant at Chicago), was the brand new coach then and he wanted to coach veterans—Kevin McHale and Larry Bird types. He just wanted to be there and give a few directions and blend a bit of talent. He wasn't prepared to do the disciplining or build the foundation of the team that we needed.

And so inevitably, it got ugly. At one stage, guard Pooh Richardson got to a point at time outs where he'd say to coach, 'f... off, it's your fault not mine.' Jimmy would take him out of the game and that was a bummer of a situation to be around. We were continually losing and the day-to-day existence was difficult. It sounds a bit weak and you do control your own destiny, but it became a pattern for the team. That's why the Wolves have struggled, there's a mentality of 'Jeez, we can't win and we can't get this going.'

It was the first time in my career I saw players talk back to the coach, players missed practice more than they missed meals, Christian (now at Atlanta) would do that, so too did JR Rider (recently traded to Portland), very frequently. Players simply had no respect. Christian or JR would miss a practice once a month or every couple of weeks. Guys missed planes. That's a $5000 fine, but Rider's making $4–5 million a year. Big deal!

The contrast between the Wolves and the Bulls was evident from the first day and now into my third full season with the Bulls, I wonder just how anything got accomplished at the Wolves at all. The owners of the Timberwolves made their money through health clubs and had built a gym at the bottom of the Target Center, called the Arena Club. One of the lures of membership obviously was that the players practised there and they built the court to be visible from almost any point within the club.

We would work out to an audience, a lot of girls on stationary bikes and stairmasters, you know, jiggle, jiggle, trying to be seen. It was just an unprofessional environment. The weights room and courts were an inconvenient walk from the showers and our private locker rooms, so it became an effort for guys to lift weights or do anything extra—all the little things it was going to take to make us better.

I got to Chicago and we have our own private practice facility, all self-contained and separate from where we play, which is nice. Guys are getting in early, guys are staying late working out, guys are staying all summer. I like to say it's a corporate culture of success. You get into a situation where people are positive and that rubs off.

By nature that's how I am anyway, but perhaps being young and pretty impressionable,

I got completely overwhelmed by the negative corporate culture at Minnesota

and by the time I got traded I was trying to figure out how to extract myself from it. Once I got to Chicago, all the positive side of me came to the fore with good players around me. It was just getting rid of the bad habits I learned at Minnesota for the first year or so and it's been steady progress ever since.

At times at Minnesota I wondered, 'The money's great, but I'm not enjoying myself'. Do you keep doing it for the money, is that why you do it? It was a great example of how money doesn't make you happy, not even 1.7 million American dollars my second year. We had the fancy car and cool pad but we were still in the Arctic tundra of Minnesota.

When we first arrived (after my contract holdout) at Thanksgiving, they had a 14-inch snow storm, then another foot at Halloween. People were sticking broom handles into the snow looking for their cars—that's what we'd landed in. Kelly had lived in the balmy heat of New Mexico all her life and I had four years there, plus I grew up in Perth. I'd always wondered what 'wind chill factor' actually felt like. It was a big adjustment.

We rented a big old mansion, the first thing available, and I didn't really have a very good understanding of money. I'd been living off $335 a month for four years at college, and now had this $1m signing bonus—a million dollar cheque—which was upfront money. Then for six months, every two weeks, you get paid the balance. So we rented this house, a four storey, stone mansion with beautiful timber staircases. It was probably a silly thing to do, but it was near a big park which was great for sledding, something we did a lot of, even though we weren't supposed to as a condition of our contract.

The house wasn't quite haunted, but it had all the hallmarks of the Addams Family mansion. One night we came home after a big night and Kelly unloaded a scream normally saved for a *Psycho* movie. Now girls have screamed at me before, but I hesitantly glanced back over my head and there was a bat the size of my hand sticking to the frame of the door. We worked out we had bats living in the basement. I caught the poor little bastard and threw him outside in to the snow and he was still there in the morning, frozen stiff. I felt horrible about that.

We did have some good times though. I had an endorsement with Qantas and they gave me 10 return business class tickets for the year, and I was dealing them out to my mates enticing them to venture to Minneapolis for a couple of weeks. We wanted to enjoy ourselves. One evening Andrew Vlahov embarked on a backyard fence hurdle in the middle of the night.

Like Edwin Moses, Hoffa would dash through backyards jumping fences until he wiped out this entire picket fence two doors down and while he was trying to work out whether he was concerned or hysterical with laughter, he kept running straight to our back door. Now there was a foot of snow on the ground so it wasn't hard to follow the footsteps of the culprit. We weren't very popular in our neighbourhood. Part of the problem was we were much too social, and we had our Aussie mates there having fun, and not getting the job done. After all I was just out of college and 22 years old.

On the basketball floor, I didn't like the guys I was working with and I didn't like the team I was playing for. Really, I wasn't ready for the NBA after college.

I felt why not go back to Australia, where I love the guys that I would be playing with

like Andrew, and playing for Adrian Hurley at Perth. I love those guys and I'd love playing basketball, I'd be a happier man and I could still earn a living.

I got to a point where I asked Andrew to feel out the situation and find out what kind of money I could make with the Wildcats. This was around 1992–93, a year into my pro career. I also entertained Europe as a playing option. But never in my heart did I really come close to quitting. I think I had too much pride and wanted to do it too badly, the whole 'first Aussie' thing was really playing on my mind. But as I said, the summer of

LUC LONGLEY

Jerry Krause.

the second year in the pros, I was feeling depressed about it and wanting to enjoy basketball again.

At that point I recognised I had some agency in the situation and came back to Minnesota and spent the summer of 1993 working out, getting my strength up, getting back into basketball, playing the summer pro leagues, getting involved and trying to rekindle the things that had made me a great player in college (University of New Mexico). I think it was that summer of work that got me to a level where other teams like Chicago got interested in getting hold of me.

Kelly and I wanted a change. Coach Phil Jackson, general manager Jerry Krause and the whole Bulls organisation believed in me enough and gave me that chance. They came to my rescue. ○

chapter 2

finally,
a basketball lifeline

Loss after loss after loss can start to get a guy down. It stinks actually, take it from me. Life at Minnesota had become a living hell. It just wasn't working out like I'd planned. Partly my fault, I guess because I don't think I was really ready for the NBA when I was drafted. It took me some time to get my game together. But the circumstances at the Timberwolves made for a miserable existence. I had to get out.

Two and a half seasons at the Wolves, punctuated by a contract holdout, injuries and a draining losing mentality, were about to come to an end. I had a sense three days before the trade deadline in February 1994 that I might be on the move. I knew Don Nelson at Golden State had been interested in me for a long time, ever since draft day in fact, three years earlier. He liked my style of basketball and I thought if anyone was going to be out there and trying to get me, it was probably him. One of the stark realities of the NBA business though, is that you don't really get told very much, you're a commodity, rather than a partner. You're there to be bought and sold and it can be frustrating not being part of the loop.

We had a new general manager in Jack McCloskey, ex-GM at Detroit who was responsible for shaping the Pistons' back-to-back world championship teams in the late 80s, and the word was out that something was percolating in the Wolves' front office. I had spoken to my agent, Lee Fentress from Advantage International, and he also felt that it appeared I was the one on the chopping block.

LUC LONGLEY

I was the next piece of meat up for grabs.

Many players dread trade talk, but honestly, I was quite excited about the prospects of being packed off to a new city.

Moves had to be made and Jack was the man to pull the trigger. I was his final card to play as I was the last guy in the starting five with any trade value that he hadn't brought in himself or had drafted. The others were Christian Laettner, Isaiah Rider, Chuck Person and Michael Williams. Off-guard Doug West was an original Timberwolf and having a good season (14.7ppg), and the front office was keen to keep him. He was the pet of the franchise. Everyone else besides me was one of Jack's boys.

Jack liked me and the previous summer (August/September 1993) I had worked hard, made a lot of improvement and people around the league were becoming much more interested in me. Jack was under a lot of pressure to make some changes because we were still losing after he'd brought all his own people in. The Wolves franchise won 29 games in their second season and things were looking up, but they'd never eclipsed the 30-win barrier. It was obvious a deal was needed, even if it was only seen as a token effort to make the team better, and the rumours were hot that I would be on my way. One rumoured deal that surfaced had me and Horace Grant going to New Jersey in exchange for Derrick Coleman.

But I'd had it with the deep freeze, I wanted to go out west, soak up some rays, feel good about life. I fit in much better in the west of the United States, it's a little bit more laid back and it's an easier going environment for me, whereas the east is a little bit uptight, a little bit old school, very big-city orientated—plus it's got the horrible weather. The west is a bit more modern, more progressive and I thought 'Great, let's get out on the west coast'. I thought for sure the Warriors, with Nelson at the helm, would trigger the move and get me to town.

Yet the thing working against me was that traditionally, Western Conference basketball is up-and-down, fast break, athletic ball and Eastern Conference hoops is more grind-it-down, pound-it-inside, defensive-minded, sort of New York Knicks basketball. So I was really more suited to the east, but I had my fingers crossed.

Two days before the deadline, 21 February, I called my core group of mates in Minnesota that included a substantial Australian contingent that I'd plugged in to. I lived right downtown, smack in the hub of the city's restaurant and bar district, my wife Kelly and I had a warehouse two blocks from the Target Center. I called up my friends, and said

FINALLY, A BASKETBALL LIFELINE

'Let's go out to dinner, it could happen at any time, I've got a feeling I could be traded.' They discounted the news of the trade and I could understand their rationale. At that stage, people were starting to support me, I was becoming a crowd favourite in Minnesota and beginning to make progress.

That evening before dinner, Kelly and I were running late as usual, I was in the shower and the phone rang. Kelly stormed down the stairs, stuck her head in the shower and said excitedly 'Luc, Luc, it's Jack!' She was pumped, she thought we were going to San Francisco. I got out of the shower, dripping wet, and stuck a towel around my waist and took the phone. I heard a very solemn voice say 'Luc, it's Jack.' His nickname was Trader Jack because he was renowned for making trades. 'I've got good news and bad news for you. Obviously we've made a deal for you,

Arriving at the office.

it wasn't easy but we've made a deal.'

Things were looking up. 'That's the good news right, what's the bad news?' He didn't think that was very funny, but he said

'The good news is, it's to Chicago.'

For a split second there was nothing. There was a void in my mind. I was sort of bummed out. I mouthed the word 'Chicago' to Kelly and we both felt like our dog had died. But five seconds later, I thought 'Hang on, mum just got a job there, my best friend is there and it's not a bad team'. Suddenly, it's like you bloody ripper. I said 'Thanks Jack, great, that's terrific', and that was it.

Making the trade was tough for Jack. He indicated without saying as much that he thought he was doing me a favour. He said 'You'll really enjoy it, they have a great coaching staff, a good program.' I think Jack quite liked me and I really think he knew he was doing something good for my career, as well as getting him off the hook because he was in a position where he had to make a trade. Trading me for Stacey King made him look very bad in the end and surprise, surprise, he's not the general manager there anymore. But at the time he thought it was a good deal.

As we left the house for dinner and knowing friends and media would be calling, Kelly hastily left a phone message that built to an excitable crescendo 'If you want to get hold of Luc, you'd better get hold of him soon, because we're off to Chicago.' And in the background I yelled out 'Da Bulls'. That came through very clearly on the message and of course the radio and TV stations did call when we were out having a few beers with my Australian mates. So what got broadcast around Minnesota was the phone message of us in a celebratory mood yelling 'Da Bulls'.

We ran down to the restaurant with great big beaming grins on our faces. And of course our mates didn't understand how we felt about it. They were disappointed, really bummed out. 'What are you happy about, man? You're leaving us,' they said. But it was a giant sigh of relief for us. I was now in to a winning situation with established players, and if nothing else, it was a change of scenery. I had been bogged down in Minnesota with a lot of disruptive pressures. ○

chapter 3

Bulls mystique, what's that?

I felt quite awkward when I first came to the Bulls. They were fresh from three straight championships, but had been rocked by the retirement of Michael Jordan six months earlier. It was a very storied franchise but I hadn't read those stories. I'm a basketball player not a fan. I didn't watch the Bulls. I didn't pay much attention to Scottie Pippen or Horace Grant. I felt when I got there I was supposed to know what goes on, that they were living legends in their own minds (and rightly so). But I hadn't subscribed to the whole Bullsmania and yet when I got there, I was impressed with the professionalism of the players and work ethic.

The NBA, and particularly the Bulls, were never a focus for me as a kid

and therefore this wasn't the realisation of a lifelong goal. I hadn't grown up with the whole USA basketball culture, dreaming to one day make the 'show', emulating the feats of greats like Kareem Abdul-Jabbar and Bill Walton. This was largely because there wasn't any television coverage of American basketball.

Unlike today, you couldn't find basketball magazines in Australia, certainly not American magazines. You had to go to Jim Kidd's (a sportstore), and you had to go to the specialty stores to find good basketball shoes. Then you might get lucky at times, Converse may

11

LUC LONGLEY

Worst seat in the house.

have sent them a Larry Bird poster, but getting your hands on them was tougher than making a hook shot back then.

There was a basketball shop under the grandstand at Perry Lakes and they had Converse socks, Magic Johnson posters, that was it. I wasn't exposed to the NBA and I didn't know anything about the league, so I was never a fan of it. I was a ballboy for the Wildcats when they

BULLS MYSTIQUE, WHAT'S THAT?

started in the NBL, dad was playing for them in the league's formative days and that was my basketball mecca.

Growing up, my heroes were Ray Borner and Larry Sengstock. I thought Ray was the prototypic big man, he could shoot the jump shot, run the floor, he was versatile. My basketball goals grew as I got older, but making a state team and then an Australian team were the things I was thinking about.

Whether hoopin' on my own or with mates, I wasn't Larry Bird shooting over Magic Johnson, I was Ray Borner pulling up over Larry Sengstock in the backyard, or at Perry Lakes, shakin' and bakin' as a young teenager. They were my basketball role models.

I got a lot of sporting inspiration from Aussie rules football players as much as anyone, Bruce Doull was one of my heroes as a kid, The Flying Doormat, there was no-one like him.

I loved the Blues as a kid, although now I'm a Dockers fan since I did grow up in Freo. But Doull was the man and I used to watch him play on *The Winners*, he did all the dirty work and that was the attraction. Unappealing, yet appreciated. Last season in the Finals against Seattle, I used The Doormat as my alias at the hotel. 'Checking in sir?' the front desk attendant asked. 'Yes thanks, Bruce Doull, D-O-U-double L.' Bruce won a couple of VFL premierships, but I bet he never realised he won a ring with Michael as well.

I guess basketball was always going to happen for me. Dad is 6'10" and played for Australia, mum's 6'4" and played for the state. I grew up killing time on the back courts of Perry Lakes. I didn't really join a club until I was 11 or 12. I was a rugby league player before that. I wasn't pushed in to basketball and wasn't pushed once I was in it either. My two younger brothers are Griff, 23, who is is 6'8" and Sam who's 6'11" at 24. We all began playing at the same time at the Police and Citizens youth club in South Fremantle.

They've got other interests which is nice for a family balance. Griff's now at university in Perth and building his own house, while Sam has immersed himself in the world of theatre and has started his own comedic theatre company which is doing quite well.

It's funny. I've only ever played two games for Perth and that's one of the reasons I'd like to get back and have a go some day.

But more than anything, when my dad's team beat the Ellis brothers from Stirling, that was a season highlight for me. The Ellis gang of Glenn and Mike, even Brett, were the enemy because it was the Perth Pacers as they were known then, against the Stirling Senators. I like the Ellises, but they were the bad guys back then and that was my basketball focus. One of the most satisfying moments came when I was younger and playing state league during my college summers.

LUC LONGLEY

When I was a ballboy for the Wildcats, Glenn Ellis used that line out of *Cool Hand Luke*, the movie; 'Got your mind right Luke?', you know the one. I was always forgetting to give someone a drink, or messing up somehow and I'd hear it. 'Got your mind right Luc?' I was a sensitive young kid and I hated it. One day I was out sweeping the court at Perry Lakes with one of those big double brooms every gym in the nation once used, and I went arse over the handle bars. It got caught, I don't know how, but I got too close. People were getting ready for the game, it was a big game against Geelong, Cal Bruton was in town, and the stands were filling up.

I went over the handle bars and I was crushed. I'd never felt so small, despite my emerging frame. Everyone's trying to be polite, not laugh too much, but I could tell everyone had seen it. God, I was on centre stage. And out of nowhere I cop it: 'Got your mind right Luc?' It was Glenn Ellis. I was stunned and humiliated.

So some years later, Andrew Vlahov and I were playing for the Redbacks in the SBL final and who do we meet? The Stirling Senators and the Ellis boys. By this stage I'm already seven foot and playing good basketball just before my senior year at New Mexico. I enjoyed coming home in the summer and got a few games in to stay in shape and hook up with the boys. And who should be jumping centre tip against me with defeat in his eyes—6'3" Glenn Ellis.

With revenge in mind I glared down and put it on him. 'Got your mind right Glenn?' We beat them by 50 for the SBL title. That's still one of my best stories. Just that moment alone was worth bottling because that was something that had stuck with me since I was a kid.

It was the Perth basketball scene that was important to me growing up, not the Bulls and the NBA. So when I got to Chicago and people said it must have been a dream, I actually felt a little bit lost. I didn't have that overwhelming awe of the situation, but that may have endeared me to the boys a bit more. I knew they were good, however, and I was psyched about that, but they weren't my cultural icons. ○

chapter 4

inflated

Chicago sports fans had been left with a basketball void, a hole left by the retirement of Jordan that was so big, not even his bank account could fill it.

We made the second round of the 1994 play-offs and were knocked out by New York in a tough series. The next year, we lost Horace Grant through free agency to Orlando and the power base of the east shifted to Florida. Back-up forward Scott Williams also took the cash and court time offered by Philadelphia and we were weak in the front court.

Scottie Pippen had been feuding with management and demanded to be traded. It nearly happened with Seattle, a deal which would have made Shawn Kemp a Bull. But once Sonics owner Barry Ackerley heard the fan backlash on one of his Seattle radio stations, he vetoed the deal and Scottie stayed put. Had Scottie been traded, it's doubtful Michael would have returned to the Bulls.

The rumours were running hot. Around about a month before

Michael finally returned, he came back to practice with us several times. He'd showed up to practice in the past, but this time it was obvious he was around more regularly. We could certainly feel his presence. A lot of the guys, and me included, could sense he was trying to get a read on how good the team was and if he wanted to come back. When he did come to practice it was great. It was fun, lighthearted and he went head-to-head with Scottie. In fact that was some of the best basketball you could ever see. It was the two premier players in the game using each other as a basketball yardstick.

At the time, Michael's practices did a lot for our team, it got us fired up in the middle-to-end of the season when you're desperately searching for things to get fired up about. That's when the season is starting to drag on, through February and March. But we were playing very well and when he started showing up it started to kick in and we were playing some of our best basketball at practice. We were working very well as a team, distributing the ball, had the triangle (offence) down, just had everything going. We weren't sure how good we were going to be. Beating an Orlando in the play-offs was still an unknown.

News of Michael's potential return brought an onslaught of distractions. We were under siege from the media, we couldn't get in to practice, the parking lot was jammed with broadcast trucks and remember, this was still speculative. The circus had fully returned and we didn't know what was going on because Michael hadn't made up his mind. Most of the team was wondering 'what the f.... is going on?' But Michael put our minds to rest as we were coming off the practice floor one day by excitedly jumping up on my back and announcing 'I'm with you guys'. It was unnofficial but it carried a lot of weight.

March 17, 1995. BANG! Michael's two-word statement said it all:

'I'm back'

and the media circus suddenly doubled in magnitude. The media crush was bigger than the play-offs, because it was a huge novelty. Anything at all was big news. When we ran out in his comeback game at Indiana, coach strategically put Michael in the middle of the line. I was right behind him, I think another big guy was right in front of him and we ran through a gauntlet of media, banks of cameras on either side.

As soon as Michael ran by, the media tried to pinch in and follow him on to the court, and we're talking guys with heavy cameras on their shoulders. I must have run over three or four cameramen, just stampeded them, because they were jumping in. I reckon the whole team ran over them because there was still half the team behind me.

For the first home game with Michael the stands were full almost an hour before the game began, which was very unusual. What was even more unusual was that everyone was standing, silent and waiting. When he ran out on to the court the crowd exploded, and so did thousands and thousands of flash bulbs. A funny sidelight was that my mother was in the audience and she couldn't see him. She was wondering why everybody was making a fuss when MJ wasn't even there. He was there alright, but he was a good head and shoulders shorter than me and slight. She hadn't spotted him. She had expected a far more imposing physical presence, having not seen him in the flesh before.

Michael gives Ron an encouraging hand.

LUC LONGLEY

It was always going to be tough for Michael and the players. Michael had so much pressure on him, 'The world's greatest player' had returned and he expected so much from himself. He'd only had two weeks of basketball and, though I don't think he really admitted it, his body wasn't in Jordan-shape. He would often glide to the basket and his memory would say 'I can jump from here', but he would land three feet short of where he thought he'd be and have to toss up something foreign at the end of it. He couldn't finish at the rim the way he wanted.

He had built up a lot of upper body strength for swinging the baseball bat and that changed his body around. He didn't have the legs. For the championship year he was a lot leaner than at his comeback. Following the 1995 play-offs, sceptics started to speculate he was too old, over the hill, didn't have it anymore. That just got Michael more fired up, he's not the kind of guy that gets down on himself, and he got more and more intense.

Owner Jerry Reinsdorf.

No athlete can have two years off and just come back, I don't care how good you are. He wasn't playing great basketball. Practice was one thing, but we suffered as a team come game time for a while as he got back in a groove. He had to have the ball and he was shooting so much. He was 7-for-28 in his first game and we had a couple of weeks of that.

It was tough to question him because he was a basketball demi-god and it was difficult for anyone to say 'Hey, give it up Mike!' We had to let him go a little bit. Phil Jackson told Steve Kerr to tell Michael that he was open in the corner and should have got the ball for the open three. Steve shrugged his shoulders as if to say 'I'm not telling the best player in the world how to play the game.'

MJ was getting frustrated and the thing about him saying to me 'Drop another one of my passes and I'll hit you in the head with it', was purely a manifestation of his frustration, largely with himself. I'd only dropped two of his passes and he'd only been there a couple of days, but it was an outlet for him. It was unfortunate though, because with the amount of media attention around the team, it was blown right out of proportion. Tribune reporter Sam Smith, who wrote *The Jordan Rules*, took that as an indication of disharmony in the team and got a headline out of it. Sam's always looking for that sort of stuff.

At his comeback game at Indiana, when Michael tore off his sweats, he revealed the No.45 uniform, it was a masterful piece of Jordan self promotion. Every kid in America already had a 23. Now they'd need a 45.

He jokes about No.45 now and wishes he'd never done it, he reckons it brought him bad luck. By returning to No.23, I reckon it was a nice way for him to shed the skin of frustration he endured while wearing his comeback jersey.

It was the Michael who wasn't quite Michael.

'No.45 doesn't explode like No.23 used to,' said the Magic's Nick Anderson after their Game One win in the 1995 play-off series. Certainly when he got back to the famed and expeditiously un-retired No.23 for Game Two, he was himself again and averaged 33.4 points over the final five games. The number change cost owner Jerry Reinsdorf $100,000 in fines from the league.

Of course the NBA and the rest of the basketball world went nuts when Michael got off for 55 against the Knicks at their place. For good measure he hit Bill Wennington with a great pass with 3.1 seconds left for the game-winning dunk, 113-111. Michael's got enough inherent ability to get hot like that. A few days later he sidled up next to Phil and said with a smile 'I've decided to quit. What else can I do?'

Even in that game he could have had 65, but he got tired in the fourth quarter. The difference with Michael wasn't that he couldn't make particular shots or dominate at times, it was just that he wasn't ready to do it every night. But that game certainly helped him remember the Michael Jordan that he was, and is now. I suspect there was a little bit of self doubt when he first came back.

We'd never really talked about championships much as a team. Obviously it was an unwritten rule amongst the Bulls not to look

LUC LONGLEY

The reach around the block is a favourite of mine.

RUNNING WITH THE BULLS

Listening and learning at practice.

LUC LONGLEY

The court of King Jordan.

Some pre-game banter on the road.

RUNNING WITH THE BULLS

Michael displays his fabled practice intensity.

LUC LONGLEY

Playing post can attract a crowd.

towards the destination before the journey had been endured. But we began reading about it in the papers not so long after his comeback. It was thrown at us, given to us. I wouldn't go as far as saying there was resentment but certainly I felt we had done a good job up to that point without him, not that we didn't want him back. We were around .500 and I thought we were playing good basketball.

In fact we had been well below .500 basketball at one stage and climbed out of it. The Bulls became Michael and his shitkickers again and it was hard for a lot of guys to swallow. I don't mind playing second fiddle, but what I now saw was a forum for Michael to showcase his talent and it was awkward for sure. I probably didn't try to embrace him or get along with him to begin with, partly because I didn't really want to.

We sort of got our act together as a team but just didn't have it together enough against Orlando in the second round of the 1995 play-offs. I thought I did a pretty good job on Shaq in that series, but it was our offence that wasn't ready. The Magic generated a lot of fast breaks out of that. Phil didn't have the confidence in me then to guard Shaq one-on-one, we always brought over the double team, so perhaps I wasn't ready to take on a bigger load just yet.

MJ was very withdrawn from the team and I think he was very frustrated with his return. He had a lot of pressure through the incessant media attention, he was edgy with teammates, everybody. Generally, he wasn't very nice to be around. We were seeing a man under a lot of pressure. I don't think he expected his comeback to cause him so much stress. I think he was surprised it was so difficult for him to get it back together.

The Orlando series that year brought it home to roost. In the first game all we had to do was hold possession and Game One was ours. Michael had a horror stretch with a turnover, had the ball stolen by Nick Anderson and Orlando took the lead. On the next play he threw the ball away.

Magic won 94–91 and took the series 4–2. But then he used the whole series as motivation over summer to come back and redeem himself. That was his sole focal point.

After that Orlando series, I was disappointed. I thought we could do much better. I had a play in the last game against Orlando which I stuffed up with a minute to play, a blown lay-up. I thought I got fouled, they didn't call it, that sort of stuff. It got me down. I had sprained my ankle in Game Two badly, no-one really knew it though. So I had no base on that play, people say 'You should have dunked it on top of everyone', but I could barely jump off the ground. I was dragging it around like a wooden leg.

LUC LONGLEY

It was a frustrating end to the season

with the return of Michael. I was real unhappy as I felt unappreciated for my efforts. MJ just wasn't being part of the team in terms of communicating. We'd become a close team and Michael changed that dynamic a bit.

He was such a big presence in the club, larger than life, and I wasn't comfortable with it. It wasn't a big deal within the team. It was something Michael and I had to overcome. He made efforts in coming and talking to me, even apologising in one instance.

I resented his comeback at times. I didn't resent him for coming back, I just wanted him to share it more, share IT, not necessarily the ball because he's the greatest scorer of all time, but share the whole thing. I wanted him to be different to what he was, I had certain expectations of him and that wasn't what he was. It frustrated me. Perhaps if I was more of a Bulls fans and had read up on him I would have realised what he was, what he is. ○

chapter 5

a menace? no way, not my dennis

Ah Dennis. Where do you start? I was never a Dennis Rodman fan, couldn't bring myself to it. I always thought he was a product of the spoilt athlete syndrome, which is where American athletes get taken in high school and college, get handed everything on a plate, play small-time celebrity and never have to grow up. I thought Dennis was basically a kid having a tantrum. And really, there's a certain element of that still. Whether it was going to a successful dynamic or not, when he signed I knew it was going to be fun. I wasn't a big fan but at least it was going to show me a different side of the NBA and I was intrigued to see how I would get on with him.

We already had Scottie, we had Michael, we obviously needed a power forward to fill Horace Grant's void, someone to help on the boards, and when PJ said we'd signed him on 12 October 1995, five days before training camp, the overwhelming response was 'great'. I was ecstatic. It was like Phil boldly declaring: 'We're going to win the championship.' That was still six months away, but suddenly the jigsaw took a turn for the better, like when you find that elusive piece that opens up the rest of the picture.

Dennis was the very obvious piece we lacked. I'm not stupid, I could see how valuable he was going to be. I was fired up, high for days and couldn't wait for him to get to town. I was certainly prepared to give him a second chance on my judgement of him as a player.

In the past, I'd been asked to guard him and told to keep him off the boards and done a half decent job at times, but unlike the majority of the league, he and I had never had a confrontation. I looked at the antics and taking the shoes off which punctuated his turbulent times at San Antonio, but I didn't know he has a foot condition where his feet basically burn. He's airing them out, trying to cool them down. That was a misunderstanding, and I was a victim of him not telling people why he did it.

When he got to the Bulls he was really quiet, didn't say a thing, he's a really shy bloke actually—at least off camera—and he was initially around us too. It took him nearly two-thirds of the season before he was really relaxed around us and being himself. I approached him a couple of times, pointing him in the right direction, and introduced him to my security guard friend, George, who had been doing some work with me now and then.

I thought Dennis would need some security. I used George during the 1995 play-off series when the public attention got out of control. You couldn't go out, you couldn't do anything, people were just all over you, in fact pretty rude. Because of the television exposure and particularly with Michael coming back, the 1995 play-offs were the first taste I got of the high profile. If we went out to a restaurant on the road it was a nightmare, people wanted a piece of you. In Chicago it wasn't so bad because I could pick my spots, I knew where I was going and could get a back table.

So George was coming on the road with us. We hired a van and if we wanted to go to a restaurant or pub, someone like him would keep the morons away. He's a cop in Chicago, working nightshift, and had it set up in a flexible manner so he could come and do things with us. He was getting us through doors.

If we went to a packed nightclub and the line was long, he'd explain who we were. We'd be at a bar and there'd invariably be someone obnoxious in your face, drunk perhaps, telling you you're great or telling you you suck. George would ask them to leave or if needed, move them. It wasn't an epidemic but it happened enough that it was handy when he was around, plus he's a nice guy, I like his company.

George actually said to me he'd like to work for Dennis. I passed that on to Dennis and his answers back then were 'uh' and 'ugh'. 'Uh' was interested and 'ugh' was not interested. I mentioned it, he didn't say anything but a couple of weeks later he was hooked up with George. Dennis had Jack Haley (Bulls teammate, who came with Dennis from San Antonio) at that stage, as a sort of a minder. Jack was perceived by many as the only man who could control Dennis, or at least Jack had us all believe it.

He didn't come in the trade, we got him through free agency. But

A MENACE? NO WAY, NOT MY DENNIS

An unusual role reversal as the Finals come to a head.

with the Bulls being unsure of how it would go with Dennis, Jack advertised himself as someone who could help keep Dennis in line, get him to practice, get him out of bed. Little did we know that, well yes, he is often late to practice, but he's the hardest worker in terms of the number of hours he puts in, he's absolutely tireless. Jack was unnecessary in the end, but the Bulls felt they needed a friend of Dennis's to keep him in check.

At training camp, Dennis arrived and the media was all over him. There was a new sideshow in town and I think Michael thought that was terrific, he didn't resent it one bit. I think it freed MJ up to focus on his game. His comeback must have worn him out mentally with the ensuing media crush. MJ is great with the media, but there were no complaints when Dennis stole the limelight with his sunglasses, furs and wild, ever-changing coif.

LUC LONGLEY

All business.

At first though, you could sense the chill between Scottie and Dennis. There had been that animosity from the 1991 Eastern Conference finals at the height of the Pistons–Bulls rivalry when Dennis pushed Scottie off the court as he drove to the basket. It was pretty ugly, and Scottie still has the scar under his chin to prove it. It was typical Detroit Bad Boys stuff. Pip hadn't forgotten the incident, nor had he forgiven Dennis. He said he would merely 'tolerate' his new teammate. 'I don't have to like Dennis Rodman off the basketball court,' explained Pip at the time, 'as long as I like what he does on the court.'

So Pip was really distant from Dennis at first, as was Michael. But I think Dennis earned their respect pretty quickly by the way he played and practised. And it freed up Michael to do less, suddenly everything was less of a hassle with Dennis around. Dennis took on a huge profile in the team and that was great. Scottie and Michael, who were the leaders of the team, immediately recognised his value. I did too. But I didn't know I would become such good mates with Dennis.

Dennis was a loner, real quiet, and to break the ice I had to get into Dennis's environment to foster any sort of communication. I had to go out to a Dennis-type bar, if you know what I mean. That's what Dennis does,

Dennis likes sleaze, Dennis likes sex, Dennis likes anything bawdy.

It's a good chuckle now and again.

That first invitation to party came from Dennis. Out of the blue it's like 'Let's go out' and I said 'great' and I jumped in a limo. That's a standard for Dennis. When we're on the road and we rock up to the hotel in the team bus, there's often two or three limos out the front if we don't have to play that night. That means the boys are going out; Michael, Scottie, Dennis, the big-timers. I don't go out that much. The only times I do go out with Dennis really are when I feel like a bit of a walk on the wild side.

So a few of the boys—Jud Beuchler and Jack were there—end up at one of Dennis's hang-outs. It didn't take long before it started to get rowdy. I dropped a couple of kamikazes (shooters) with Dennis and pretty soon I figured out what makes him tick. I hadn't known him long and this was the breakthrough night in many respects. Dennis just likes to have fun, he's high energy and he doesn't sleep much. You've got to be prepared to stay for a little while. He had a bad marriage and puts no stock whatsoever in relationships or marriage. His whole world is rapid turnover without responsibility. I'll pierce my nose if he gets married again. It's just not him.

Dennis attracts weird people, the freaks, way out dudes, transvestites, flaming homosexuals and straights. There's always plenty of tattoos and body piercing, and everyone has serious attitude. It's actually quite fun. Dennis is often looking for someone to hang out with. I'll hook up with him sometimes, but not a lot. When we go out, it's usually a place in Chicago called the Crowbar, a very underground, Gothic sort of a joint. Coincidentally, it's where we'd end up after the championship game.

When you're out with Dennis, be prepared for a show.

That night went a long way to developing a solid off-court bond and a great on-court relationship. Once Dennis likes you, once he's with you, Dennis will do anything for you, he's a great guy to have as a mate and that came through on the court, where our rapport was great, we were always paired up. He was helping me on defence, and likewise, I

LUC LONGLEY

Our bad boy with his bad toy.

was covering his arse. It was one of those situations where it was obvious we could work well together on the court and he started to build a respect for me.

I say I'm the anchor of the defence. While Scottie and Michael are the Dobermans patrolling the perimeter, I'm back protecting the safe. Yet I know I can go out of the lane to contain some penetration and there's no way Dennis is going to allow somebody to scramble behind me for a lay-up. He'll knock them out before they do, so they don't even try it. It's like going into battle with a Tyrannosaurus Rex every night. When he's on your side, he's awesome.

I knew I could gamble at the defensive end, try to front the post, go for the steal, or double team and trap because Dennis cared so much about protecting my back and being there. Even if it meant getting dunked on now and again or looking bad, he didn't care. A lot of guys in the league won't do that. It doesn't matter if they're a mate or not, if you get there late, you risk being on the wrong side of a dunk poster. But Dennis is always prepared to do it and subsequently he's in a few posters. The essence of our team defence was no-one was afraid to fail.

Our relationship grew stronger as I began to know him better. Hours on the court playing together helped foster a mutual respect. I play hard and physical, I play how I need to play, though I'm not overtly physical. Dennis thrives on overt physicality. He lives very close to the practice facility because, basically, he lives in the gym. They might as well give him a room.

Because of his nocturnal habits, he's not always there first thing in the morning, but he'll be there well after everyone has left, he'll come back in the afternoon and maybe again in the evening. He had a specially made-up security card so he can get in 24 hours, whereas for everyone else as far as I know, it's strictly 7am–7pm. He probably gets back from bars and clubs and lifts weights, I don't know. He just can't get enough.

There's nothing too glamorous about Dennis's existence really, it's fairly basic in many ways. He lives in a house that no-one else in the NBA would even look at. It's a small brick, suburban, standard two bedroom, whatever. Not even a heated garage attached to it. He has a big pick-up truck he parks out the front. Granted, he does keep his toys back at home in Texas, where his base is.

But in Chicago, he doesn't even sleep on his bed, he sleeps on the floor. Hey, maybe he just can't find his bed when he comes home, I don't know. His house is threadbare. Even when the Bulls finally signed him for close to $9 million a year, he has said he was going to give most of it to his daughter anyway.

He's full of surprises, no doubt about that. How about the book opening? It wasn't enough just to put a tell-all book out, but he ensured the world was looking on when he launched it too.

Only Dennis could get away with the silver hair, make-up and pink feather boa.

You can only sit back and say 'Yep, that's Dennis'. He backed that up by bluffing the world in to thinking he was getting married, only he was the bride, dolled up in a veil, floor length white wedding gown, simply gorgeous. It was just another book signing gimmick and another extension of the entertainer that's wrapped up inside that toned, tattooed torso. You've got to hand it to him. It takes real guts to do the things he's doing of a gender-bending nature in a world of professional sports where macho rules. He's extending and pushing the boundaries of what is acceptable.

LUC LONGLEY

The Worm's book signing brought out the best in his cross-dressing career.

D Rod's post game workout.

He's posed nude for *Playboy* and dons a black leather number with a parrot perched on his shoulder for *Sports Illustrated*. And if he's not wearing a different hat each time he gets on the team bus, there's something wrong. He has a fashion designer make him up wild hats, big Dr Seuss, *Cat in the Hat*, leopard skin numbers that have become synonymous with Dennis in the past 12 months.

The thing that amazes me most about him is that after a game, he doesn't shower, but gets straight on the stationary bike or treadmill for half an hour, then ices his knees while lifting weights. When he's done, he throws his track pants on inside out, puts on Bergenstock sandals, leather jacket, no t-shirt, hat and walks out the door. By that time the media's gone, they can't wait for him because it takes an hour for him to finish working out. His metabolism needs the work. I reckon he's addicted to his own adrenalin.

Early in the pre-season, Dennis was gas-bagging to the papers something along the lines of

'I want to teach Luc how to streetfight, I want him to be a tough hombre, me and Luc are going to kick some ass.'

LUC LONGLEY

Tempers flared early in the pre-season, a $25,000 fine and a one-game suspension.

I didn't read it, in fact I didn't even know about it. The next night we're playing Washington in a pre-season game in Chicago against the over-paid and over-rated Chris Webber, who, as you might have guessed, I don't like. He's what I thought Dennis was, a spoilt product of the basketball system.

We were going at it all night and Webber took a cheap shot. I responded and gave him a cheap shot back. He snapped by pushing me in the back, so I clobbered him and we got in to a brawl. I had him in a headlock, and was giving him everything I had.

I was quite happy to do it. I got a one-game suspension and lost $25,000 in fines and game payments. That was money well spent and I'd do it again for sure. I didn't want someone like that, or anybody that matter, to have his way or even think he can. I've had several fights in five years of NBA basketball, and have them consistently more than my teammates.

It's funny, people in the NBA don't perceive me as soft, it's only the Australian media that does because they don't see the day-to-day. I had three fights my rookie year—James Donaldson and Sam Bowie

A MENACE? NO WAY, NOT MY DENNIS

come to mind—because players thought they could have their way with me. I guess it would be like your first day in prison, you have to make a statement there and then.

So Dennis has just told the papers he wanted me to be this way and it was terrible timing, all of sudden they think Dennis has made me do it and he probably thought the same thing. It got to a point where I elbowed Dennis in the face in a later game and he whacked me on the butt, like 'Good on ya'. That's what he wants, he's one of the old Pistons bad boys, he wants overt aggression. I tend to get the job done with less of that than most.

Underneath all the hooha and gusto on court, what people don't know about Dennis is that he's a loyal guy, he cares about his friends and looks after his people. And he loves kids, particularly Steve Kerr's son Nick. He's always giving him gifts when Nick comes in the locker room, sunglasses, posters or whatever people send to him, he gives them to Nick. He loves them, can't get enough of kids.

Dennis recognises the NBA is theatre. He's legitimate, he is what he is, but he's hamming up his part, he's the ultimate entertainer. He's actually quite thoughtful and believe it or not, he's thought about a lot of the things he's said. A lot of it is scripted, but by no-one else other than Dennis. I was asked this year who's pulling Dennis's strings and I said, 'I don't think anyone is, it's just a big tangle'. He doesn't always know what's happening or what's coming next.

He's no big talker either. While there's plenty of stories to be told, like his relationship with Madonna, much of the time it will be Jack Haley telling the stories with Dennis chuckling away in the corner. It's all true, but Dennis isn't one to hold court and tell a story, he's pretty restricted in what he says to us, although he's more open with the cameras. But all those stories gave Jack something to hang his hat on, it gave Jack a personality.

A former Prince with wife Mayte Garcia.

Dennis does enjoy the spotlight and big-time personalities love to hang with him. Dennis is a big Pearl Jam fan and is good mates with Eddie Vedder. He also presented the Red Hot Chilli Peppers with No.91 jerseys, which they wore for a 7 March concert this year at the United Center.

LUC LONGLEY

Having to fight Dennis for the rebound.

That spotlight can get Dennis in hot water though. One of the things that gets Dennis in trouble, is that he refuses to hold anything back, he refuses to not say what he thinks. He's no diplomat. He says the wrong thing at the wrong time, all the time.

People talk about him building himself up to explode, an accumulated stress. But he doesn't accumulate any stress, he wears it right on his shirt, and if he's feeling bad, he's feeling bad, if he's feeling good, he's feeling good. There's no hiding anything. And while he's obviously got some things deep inside him he talks about, his actual emotions and responses to things are as pure as anyone I've ever met.

With that in mind, when Dennis was trashing former Spurs teammate David Robinson, he meant it. It's no secret he seriously dislikes

A MENACE? NO WAY, NOT MY DENNIS

Robinson. Dennis often felt unappreciated there and believed the Admiral went missing at play-off time and that was the reason San Antonio never advanced to the championship series.

From what I can gather, the story goes that after Robinson was named MVP in 1994, he gave everyone on the team a $5000 watch, the best you can get, with their names engraved on the back. Jack Haley still wears his. Dennis left his in the locker room, he didn't want it. The trainer grabbed it and gave it back to him. Then he left it on the plane. Someone else grabbed it and gave it back to him thinking he was simply forgetting it. In the end, because it kept re-appearing as it had his name on the back, he gave it to some ballboy and said 'Here, keep it'.

He didn't want the watch because he didn't feel appreciated by David, he felt largely responsible for David winning the MVP and didn't feel the fact was recognised by Robinson at all. Jack told us this, but all these stories were told in front of Dennis. It's Jack's act, but I know it to be true. I think that was to illustrate the point Dennis doesn't lend much credence to material goods, like the house, although he asked for and got a fat contract for this year. But hey, he deserves it. What he cares about is respect and his teammates. It was less important to him to have a nice watch, than it was that people understood how he felt.

So Dennis wears his emotions on his sleeve and when he snaps and head-butts a referee, it's raw anger. When Dennis feels he's been cheated, he responds angrily. I'm different. I might be pissed off about it, but I'll remember that referee or if someone gives me a cheap shot, I'll keep my eye on him so I can get a shot at him later. It's not that way with Dennis.

He's not a calculating, brooding guy at all. If the ref pisses him off, if he feels the ref cheated him, he'll tell him, he'll head-butt him, that's why he gets tech fouls, that's why he gets thrown out. He puts it all out there. That's why he gets in to so many confrontations with people. He doesn't have the ability to put it aside and keep it for later. He responds to it. Boom!

That's how I missed him on the head-butt at New Jersey. There were several other occasions last season that I dragged him away from referees. First of all, I'm one of the only blokes that is big enough to, but secondly, we get on all right. Yet sometimes I wonder. I thought he was going to have a go at me a couple of times by that look in his eye. You grab him and look in his eyes and it's like 'Who the f... are you?' He's angry. He hasn't hit me yet and I told him if he did, it was going to be on. That's a bluff. I'm just trying to discourage him.

I've told him in no uncertain terms, 'I'm doing you a favour mate, you hit me for doing you a favour and I'm right back atchya'. He thought

35

that was great. He'd probably love for me to hit him. He loves to be hit. If there's a choice of going left, getting an elbow in the nose and maybe a rebound, or right and more than likely get a rebound and no-one is there, he'll go left just to nail it, he can't get enough.

I think he's masochistic. He loves the pain, loves to work out, loves to get hit. The team owes Dennis a lot for just how much he puts in. It's partly because of his physical condition, he's 35 years old, not an ounce of fat on him, he's a machine, a great physical specimen.

Before Dennis arrived we out-rebounded opponents by one. After he got here that stat went up by six boards, that's six possessions, and potentially 12 points. Surprise, surprise. We scored 105.3ppg and had a 12-point differential on our opponents every night on average. Dennis averaged 14.9 rebounds a night for us and just 4.8 shots. Subsequently it can be tough getting a board on this team.

In 59 of the 64 regular season games Dennis played for us, he was our leading board man. And he's only 220 pounds.

He has no regard for his body, only for the ball.

He averaged 5.66 offensive boards last year, best in the league. It's that effort that demoralises a team as much as a three-pointer.

Back to the head-butt. I was watching Dennis' face and he was incensed, talking to ref Ted Bernhardt, and so I circled around him. But I wasn't in a hurry because he's so open with his emotions, I thought he was an easy read. In actual fact he was fakin' me out so he could get to Ted because he saw me coming. He gave me the old smile and 'I'm cool' look, but he's still stepping towards Ted, so I thought I'll still keep my eye on him and Boom! He released it, then I went and got him.

That's when I was getting ready to be hit. He was looking at me like he was going to have a go at me. I was like 'Whoa'. That might have been good or it might have got him more pissed off, but it should have got me more pissed off at him because it was really bad for the team at the time. He copped a $20,000 fine and six-game suspension, which would have cost him close to a quarter of a million in salary. Scottie was already out nursing an assortment of back, ankle and knee injuries. Dennis apologised to the team which is unlike him. With that, he showed he felt he'd let us down because he cares so much about winning and his teammates. I'm stoked they re-signed him because he does care about this team.

Example. At Chicago's Grant Park, the Bulls had a championship gathering rather than the traditional parade. The place was really rocking,

A MENACE? NO WAY, NOT MY DENNIS

you could feel the energy, the 250,000 fans there on a Tuesday morning were super devout Bulls fans. When it got to Dennis to say some words, his whole speech was: 'Thank you Scottie for accepting me. Thank you for letting me be part of this team.'

It was a direct reference to the pushing incident in 1991 that attracted national headlines. But that's Dennis. At his glory moment, right when everybody was looking at him, he gave it up to someone else. Whether you agree with his politics or his antics, you have to appreciate his candidness.

I think Michael really likes him but he's wary. They are very different. Michael's very clean cut, always dressed immaculately, very socially and politically correct, right on the money, the sort of the elder statesman of the league. So he and Dennis aren't necessarily a pair, but I think Michael gets a kick out of it, Dennis might almost be his alter ego, something MJ would like to be now and then, but simply can't.

Dennis often gets a hand on what's mine.

The Atlanta Olympics were a perfect example of Dennis Rodman Inc. and his need to be around people and just having fun. Dennis turned up to the USA–Croatia game and the stadium went nuts. Fans flooded the aisles as Dennis took his seat, wanting to touch him, take his photo, or maybe get an autograph.

I was in town commentating for Channel 7 and caught up with him after the game and even interviewed him for 7. 'So Dennis, you're in charge tonight, what's up?' I asked him, resplendent as he was in Oakley sunnies and typically rad hat. 'Well, I think we'll drink a few of these,' he answered holding up his beer to the camera, beaming a broad grin. 'You and me, we've drunk a few Foster's together.'

That night Dennis was hosting a party at the Baja Beach Club in Buckhead, north of Atlanta. Dennis usually has a number of pretty girls with him, he organises that everywhere he goes. They had roped off a portion of the club and it was the hottest ticket in town. Scores of hopefuls waited patiently behind the ropes in a vain bid to be asked to come in.

It just had this aura of exclusivity and importance. By the end of the night, though, it was madness. Dennis had closed one of the island bars, had his shirt off, as did about eight other male bar staff. They were pouring beers over each other, body slamming in the bar, knocking back shots as the crowd looked on. More theatre. More entertainment. Dennis was in his element and loving it. He WAS the party.

The public just loves Dennis. They shower him with adulation and adoration and he soaks it up. He was featured on the side wall of a massive warehouse that bordered the 94 freeway going in to town. Dennis was endorsing a men's wear store, Bigsby and Kruthers. The artwork was 32 feet high and was repainted every time he changed his hair colour. It was stopping traffic and finally had to be taken down as it was adding 30 minutes to the daily commute.

The hysteria that follows Dennis these days has grown in momentum,

but there still is only one King, one Elvis. And that's Michael.

I think if Jordan was at that Atlanta party and doing his thing, there would have been a lot more people. I don't think Dennis is in Michael's league just yet, but he's getting there. Michael's so good at not letting people know where he's going to be. He's an undercover guy, he has to be, while Dennis embraces it. Dennis doesn't like to be alone, he has to be out with people, interacting, he's a social animal. Damn, he's a predator in the social jungle.

I think he's misunderstood because he's so flamboyant, colourful and tattooed. He's had a hard life, grew up in the projects in Dallas. He got in trouble early as a kid and was adopted by a white farming family, which may explain why he hangs with white guys a lot and dates only white girls. ○

chapter 6

our zen master

The Bulls get it done on the floor, but coach Phil Jackson is really the backbone of the team, he puts it all together. And one of the remarkable feats Phil has achieved is that he's used Michael Jordan in a complete offence, he's blended him in with his teammates. He convinced Michael he was just one point of a five-point star and for the franchise to be successful, Michael had to work with those players around him and learn to make them all better.

In a league where the zone rules often mean offences are structured around one or two players, relegating the rest to stand and watch the one-on-one or two-on-two show, Phil refused to follow the leader. It was just like that at Minnesota. I was left to languish outside the three-point line and not be involved. That kind of offence allows the supremely talented players like Michael, and players a lot less talented, to get isolation plays like a post up or two-on-two situations like a screen and roll.

We have, I think, two of the most talented offensive players in the game in Scottie and Michael and yet Phil flatly refuses to run the butchered, bastardised version of basketball which is NBA isolation offences. He's won four championships now with a much more pure and whole form of basketball.

It was not only the basis of the three straight titles earlier in the 90s, but again last season. He got to know us all a lot better as the season progressed, and Scottie summed it up perfectly through the Finals. Michael was working with his teammates, the same guys he didn't feel comfortable with when he came back last season. MJ was more tolerant, and realised what we have as a team.

On the same day, when we led Seattle 3–0 in the Finals, MJ afforded the same explanation and in a way, paid tribute to Phil's perseverance. 'It took a lot of pushing of myself individually and a lot of giving of myself to understand a lot of my teammates who haven't experienced this before. I had to be patient in those circumstances. Phil helped with that, with his spiritual background and teachings.

'I'm the sort of player who is so competitive that I can really ruin a lot of players' mentalities and confidence because of the aggressive play that I like to see on the court. Phil has taught me to understand my teammates and give them a chance to gel and improve.'

Obviously Michael and Scottie were the cornerstones of the offence, but it's a system that includes and utilises the other players. I've called it an equal opportunity offence. That's one of the reasons I was bored playing in Minnesota where there was no equal opportunity. I wasn't involved. It's also one of the reasons I became a pretty good defensive player there—because that was the end of the floor I got to play.

I came to Chicago and Phil got me involved immediately. Just days after my trade, Bill Cartwright got injured. I started, and in his absence had three or four games scoring in the mid teens. I got to touch the ball, move the ball. That's Phil's biggest success and that's why he's able to bring guys like me and Steve Kerr into his program, he uses us right and makes us flourish. He's always praised for getting the most out of players and I think that's because he gives them an opportunity with his offence, as well as his coaching and philosophies that bring the best out of people.

He was brought up by parents who were Pentecostal ministers. He grew up in the 60s and was influenced by eastern religion and calls himself a Zen Christian. He's given me books on Zen to read, the underlying theme being 'clear the mind and open the heart', and he preaches that at practice. There was a message on our notice board in the locker room which I think is very Zen-like and that is

'The Journey is the Reward'.

That was a quote from a book Phil had given us all to read the previous year labelled *The Little Zen Handbook*. He used that as his battle cry in the last half of the season as the media and the public began to forecast an imminent championship. Obviously that was our goal and focus, but we still had a lot of work at hand, we still had to win games, go out every night, get through the season battling injuries. People were asking 'What's it going to be like winning a championship?' and

OUR ZEN MASTER

The look of a shepherd.

LUC LONGLEY

Phil in work mode with Jim Cleamons (now Dallas head coach) working the flock.

Phil's point was 'Hey, it's great fun now, we're doing it now, the journey is the reward and this is when you have to appreciate it.'

We were up 1–0 in the championship series against Seattle and he brought it to our attention again in the film room at our practice facility at Deerfield. 'What that means is, if we win three more games and become NBA champions, our reward is not necessarily a ring, or a payroll cheque, or locker room champagne celebration, but the joy of the journey itself. And the journey is not over yet.' That was very valuable for all of us and a particular focus of Phil's.

Yes, the journey was long, but it was never a chore. What I've noticed in the past, is that people start ripping days off their calendars as a countdown to the end of the season. This year we had so much fun we had no countdown, we didn't want it to end.

I guess that fun was a by-product of belonging and knowing you were having an impact, to whatever degree that may have been. Phil gave each guy responsibility and autonomy. The offence provides autonomy on the court, it's not a robotic offence, it's an offence where you get to make decisions and react, be treated like you're an adult in a sense. Whereas with the butchered, bastardised offences, you're quite often stuck in a corner like a kid. Stay here, cut there, don't do anything.

There's much more to Phil and life than that. He doesn't put anybody in a box. The fact he's interested in guys and people, and interested in the way that people work and how they look at things, had a major bearing on my basketball well-being. It brought out the best in guys when you had someone like Phil participating in your spiritual development. He introduced us to a lot of things, we've meditated as a team, had avid discussions on aspects of life outside of basketball.

He's very much a professional, and it was all basketball to begin with. He's not the kind of guy who is going to praise you, stroke you, run up and give you a hug. He's actually quite harsh and abrupt in many ways in his communication. He just shows you over time that he cares. He's more demonstrative with actions than words. He's not going to stroke you verbally, he's not going to tell you how good you are or that he cares. He'll simply give you the opportunity as he did with me.

Phil's an oasis in the NBA. There are not many coaches in the league with his understanding, lateral thinking or compassion. I think he's a brilliant basketball coach, from an Xs and Os, offence-defence standpoint. I actually look forward to the time when I'm not playing for him and it's a little bit easier to sit down with him and have a beer and just relax with him. While it's a player-coach relationship, there are certain things you can't really do because of the disciplinary side of it. For the moment, neither of us are willing to breach that.

Being a 60s throwback in many ways, Phil often takes us back to that era with him. He's been around the Lakota Sioux Indians a lot. Almost 20 years ago he did a clinic on an Indian reservation in South Dakota and was dubbed Swift Eagle. There are a lot of Indian artefacts around our practice facility. On one wall hangs a wooden arrow with a tobacco pouch tied to it, which is the Lakota Sioux symbol of prayer. Another wall is home to a bear claw necklace, which, Phil was told, bestows power and wisdom upon its wearer.

He has the middle feather of an owl for balance and harmony, a painting that tells the story of the great mystical warrior, Crazy Horse. He's become very fond of the white buffalo too, the most sacred of animals to the Sioux, the symbol of prosperity and good fortune. He once joked that he'd like to change the Bulls logo to a white buffalo. GM Jerry Krause merely scoffed. It didn't go down very well. But think of the merchandise potential!

He gets a lot of inspiration from the Grateful Dead,

we've listened and watched a number of Grateful Dead performances as a team with various messages highlighted. In our video room there are Jerry Garcia incense burners, Grateful Dead posters, and more Indian artefacts which all have special meaning.

There's a corporate culture that's pretty well established and Phil is the one who's established it. There are a lot of identifiable features and a lot of continuity in the organisation. I think Phil provides that stability which is good for anybody to work under. As long as they know their roles, then people perform well.

That's how Phil gets his people to perform, he makes it very clear what their roles are, how they fit in, and makes them feel comfortable with it, convincing everyone along the way that they will be successful. I think he got Michael on side very early and that was extremely smart. To get Michael to subscribe to the offence that we run was paramount to the club's success.

It got to the point where Michael said he wouldn't come back if Phil wasn't there. Phil and the Bulls were still very close to going their separate ways last summer. God only knows what would have unfolded had Phil not returned. No Phil, no Michael, maybe no Bulls. I think Michael's support probably had a lot to do with the organisation re-signing PJ.

Phil subscribes to the Gestalt Theory, a German school of thought from the 1930s where the whole is always greater than the sum of the parts. I think 'Lessons from Geese' by Ryugen Fischer exemplifies that:

> **Fact 1:** As each goose flaps its wings it creates an uplift for the birds that follow. By flying in a 'V' formation, the whole flock adds 71 per cent greater flying range than if each bird flew alone.
> **Lesson:** People who share a common direction and sense of community can get where they are going quicker and easier because they are travelling on the thrust of one another.
>
> The point obviously is we help each other on offence and defence, that's the whole concept of teamwork and why I play team sport. That's what I enjoy about sport, five or 12 guys working as a unit to do something which is dynamic and being able to read each other as you go. To me that's the most fun thing in basketball, rather than a dunk or an in-your-face play. Those things are nice, but the real gratification for me, Phil and most of the guys on the team is that Gestalt union we have.

The 'Lessons from Geese' purvey such a poignant message, not only for basketball, but also in all walks of life.

> **Fact 2:** When a goose falls out of formation, it suddenly feels the drag and resistance of flying alone. It quickly moves back in to formation to take advantage of the formation.
> **Lesson:** If we have as much sense as a goose we stay in formation with those headed where we want to go. We are willing to accept their help and give our help to others.
> **Fact 3:** When the lead goose tires, it rotates back into the formation and another goose flies to the point position.
> **Lesson:** It pays to take turns doing the hard tasks and sharing leadership. As with geese, people are interdependent on each other's skills, capabilities and unique arrangements of gifts, talents or resources.
> **Fact 4:** The geese flying in formation honk to encourage those

OUR ZEN MASTER

up front to keep their speed.

Lesson: We need to make sure our honking in encouraging. In groups where there is encouragement, the production is much greater. The power of encouragement (to stand by one's heart or core values and encourage the heart and core of others) is the quality of honking we seek.

Fact 5: When a goose gets sick, wounded or shot down, two geese drop out of the formation and follow it down to help or protect it. They stay with it until it dies or is able to fly again. Then, they launch out with another formation or catch up with the flock.

Lesson: If we have as much sense as geese we will stand by each other in difficult times as well as when we are strong.

Phil's always posing questions, theories and suggestions for us to ponder. He's pretty diverse and quite dynamic, you never know quite what to expect. One of the first times I got an insight into Phil was when we were in the middle of a losing streak when I first got traded to the Bulls. In New Mexico I became aware of an Indian custom called 'smudging'. It's a bunch of sage Indians roll up in to a tight stick, like a cigar, and then they burn it, using the ashes and smoke, going round to each corner of the room, to rid the surrounds of evil spirits if something bad happens, or if someone dies, things like that.

I came in to work out early one morning and there was Phil down on the court, lighting up his sage stick trying to expel the evil spirits. It was refreshing to see a guy who believes in something enough to carry it out in real life.

During my first play-off campaign in 1994, out of the blue Phil took us on a Staten Island ferry ride in New York instead of the shootaround following a Game One loss because we were too uptight. It was the Bulls' first play-offs without Michael. Phil called the trip mind frame management. It didn't work, we lost the next game and the series.

The play-offs can bring a lot of surprises out of Phil. He enjoys taking poignant scenes from movies and splicing them into our game film, the video of opponents or breakdowns of our strengths and weaknesses. On that same Big Apple series in 1994, he used the movie *Slapshot*, a hockey movie about a team of thugs led by the Hanson brothers. The timing was made all the more amusing because we were playing New York. The lesson was obvious and the boys took it to heart.

So this year we were at home for Game One of the Eastern Conference semis against the Knicks and Steve Kerr shows up in those ugly nerd-like black-rimmed glasses with the tape in the middle, knee braces, elbow pads, pants pulled up really high, I think he had long

LUC LONGLEY

black socks on, the full Hanson brothers outfit. We circle up at centre court before practice and Steve waited until the circle was nearly full, but Phil hadn't started talking yet so guys were still messing around.

Steve then comes cruising out of the locker room. The boys died, but Phil wasn't quite so amused. It just so happened that Steve struck one of Phil's very serious days and we had a very hard practice afterwards. He ran our arses off. It was still two days before the series opener, and we'd already blown Miami out. New York uses a very aggressive, *Slapshot* sort of defence—punch them, scrap them, kick them, don't let them do anything. Steve was reminding us in his own little way.

The movies certainly work. It's just another way to emphasise a point. He used *The Shawshank Redemption* to highlight the fighting spirit of people dominated by, in that case, a prison system and by other prisoners. The scene where Tim Robbins is continually bashed by fellow inmates comes to mind, but Phil used most of the movie. The example to us was that despite the overwhelming defence we were playing against, we could identify what we had to conquer. He's used Pink Floyd's *The Wall* at times to emphasise similar things.

Phil in a demanding mood.

Phil used a line out of *Pulp Fiction* when we were up 1-0 against Seattle after blowing them out at our place and were feeling pretty good about ourselves, me in particular after scoring 14 points. He'd spliced in a killer Harvey Keitel line, 'Let's not start sucking each other's dicks just yet'. That was the punctuation. That was the last scene he played us in the video room before we went down to practice. In other words, Phil was telling us 'Yeah you've done well, but let's keep working.'

OUR ZEN MASTER

For a later game in the Seattle series he used the film *King of Hearts*, an old movie about a town that gets deserted during the war but they forget to unlock the loony bin. An English soldier comes in to check out the French town and finds it deserted, except the loonies are out running the town and all live in a fantasy world.

The soldier has to figure out how to get real information from them as opposed to the loony world they've conjured for themselves. The message Phil was giving, and it was illustrated quite poignantly in quite a few scenes in the movie, was how to run our offence against Seattle's crazed, unpredictable and unexplainable defence. We had to make sense out of the madness and find what we were looking for.

If it's not a movie in the post-season, then it's some literature through the year. I remember he gave Dennis his book, *Sacred Hoops*, and passed on *Dirty White Boys* to Bill Wennington. The teachings of Zen are always popular and so is the unpredictable, like *Beginner's Mind to Beavis & Butt-head: This Book Sucks*. He once gave former starter John Paxson *Zen & the Art of Motorcycle Maintenance*, by Robert Pirsig. Pip fessed up this year and revealed not only didn't he read the book he got, he couldn't remember its name either.

Some of the most surprising moments in my basketball career have been around Phil Jackson. Things like coming into a locker room, down 17 at half-time in Game Two to Orlando in the 1996 play-offs and Phil saying, 'We have them right where we want them' and meaning it. In this case they were beating us by overplaying the passing lanes, over-committing on the ball and we were making poor decisions. Phil meant we have them 'right where we want them' in that it would only whet their appetite more in the second half and, with the right decisions, it was a sure way of making them play right into our hands offensively.

Orlando scored 35 second-half points and coughed up the ball 12 times in the final 18 minutes. 'They were in our faces so much that all we could do was just get the ball to a teammate, much less think about putting it in the basket,' said an out-gunned Dennis Scott. We'd reversed a 38–53 half-time deficit in to a 93–88 Game Two win.

The point being is that we made the adjustments at half-time and came out and destroyed them in the second half. Phil's just very calm in the face of pressure and that rubbed off on the team. That's why we won so many games that were in the balance.

Between Phil's serene nature and Michael's brilliance, we just had great poise down the stretch.

I think Phil won us a lot of games, first, by what he implemented, and second, by instilling in the guys enough faith in themselves and each other, to just let it all hang out and do it. Some coaches who are ranting and raving on the sidelines make guys uptight and nervous. Guys get tight because they're not sure whether they are doing the right thing, not believing they should be out there—confusion reigns, ambiguity rules. But to Phil it can't be ambiguous if we are given complete autonomy within a system.

There are times when he's stern, but for the most part he guides you not by pushing or shoving, but by being alongside you and that's certainly how I respond best to coaching.

I think Phil was largely responsible for bringing me to the Bulls, I think he appreciated my skills or saw what they were and the potential for what they could be. He recognised the fact I pass the ball very well, and in the triangle offence, our signature tune, we use the post a lot as a passer.

The Bulls have seven rules of sound offence. One of them is to be able to penetrate the defence, and a post pass is a penetrating pass, it's as good as a drive or a shot. A shot is also a penetration because the ball is inside the crust, inside the skin of the defence, and from there you can either score or rebound.

The post pass is a penetrating pass because it forces the defence to collapse and so you need a post or pivot man who can distribute the ball, make sound decisions and recognise what's opening up. I think that's the primary reason why they brought me in, as well as the fact I could play some decent defence.

When I came to the Bulls I was largely playing the same basketball in terms of skills, but I had better players around me and suddenly I was looking better when a Scottie Pippen was finishing my pass with a dunk. Admittedly, Michael and Scottie made the not-so-good passes look great too sometimes. But more importantly, I was getting the opportunity—that equal opportunity—to make those passes.

In Minnesota I wasn't involved in the offence because I wasn't identified as one of the two or three guys regarded as an offensive focus. That's why teams like Minnesota have a couple of guys scoring 20, but no-one else is contributing. Whereas the Bulls are more likely to have 30 from Mike, 20 from Scottie and 10 from five other guys.

Being involved and contributing makes you want to work hard to help achieve team goals. The corporate culture created by Michael and Phil has become almost a trademark of the Bulls. We had Christmas Day off last season and the next day we got mugged by Indiana 103–97. It hurt because our whole ethic was 'Work harder than anyone, practise

OUR ZEN MASTER

harder than anyone, beat anyone'. It wasn't written, but that's the way we played.

We got killed by the Pacers, but not long after that, we crushed them 120–93. The point was, that every time a team beat us, we came back the next time and absolutely crushed them, wiped them, inflicted their biggest losses. It happened to Indiana, Orlando, Seattle, Denver, Miami and New York. Phoenix, Charlotte and Toronto were the only teams spared because we didn't play them again in the regular season. They'll hear about it this season though.

It was a demonstration of our team pride and instinct to right a wrong. After our first three losses to Orlando, Seattle and Indiana, we went on to beat them by an average 21 points after that. We lost 10 games in 1995-96 and nine times we came back and won the next game by an average margin of 16 points.

That culture, that focus was brought to practice too. You can practise hard and you can practise long, but the guys look forward to coming to practice and once they get there, they are very, very focused.

Practising fundamental skills is part of our daily routine.

We have a practice set-up where we lift weights as a team for 45 minutes. It's mostly Olympic lifting involving cleans, squats, dead lifts, stuff like that. It's complete body rhythm, strength, timing sort of lifts, rather than body building isolation type lifts that tend to make you segmentally strong but not develop your whole co-ordinated strength.

Once we hit the basketball court we spend the first 20 minutes without a basketball doing footwork drills, skipping, zig zag, roll outs, running backwards and defensive footwork. Then fundamentals—ball handling, passing drills up and down the court, just like under 16s, but Phil's theory is leave no stone unturned, go back to the basics.

That's why the Bulls always play well after a couple of practices under our belts.

We go back to fundamentals,

shell without the ball closeout drills, run the offence without the ball so the focus becomes the footwork and running. Michael, the best player in the game, Scottie and Dennis, they'll get out there and not just co-operate, but embrace it, take it seriously and concentrate on it.

Minnesota or other teams would scoff at that like 'Hey man, we're professionals'. But Phil has the guys so into it, so focused, that our practices become ultra-competitive, there's no 'Be careful he's your teammate', sort of thing. I think some of our best basketball is played at practice, Michael and Scottie go head to head, Toni and Scottie are quite fun and watch Randy Brown on Michael. Randy is one of the few defenders who can get up inside Michael and give him problems with the ball. You'll see more and more of Randy Brown this season.

Practice can be interrupted at times though. Scottie, Phil and the team's trainer sometimes bring their dogs to practice, that's two Rottweilers and a Golden Retriever. They've been known to bolt out on to the practice floor during drills. That can really mess up a guy's footwork.

In practice we have situation games where the clock is running and we have to execute certain things offensively and against pressure defence. Some days we'll get it going and be so dominant at the defensive end, we'll basically shut the scrimmage down. You'll see Michael and Scottie up the front of the press just working themselves to a lather and they'll go flat out until Phil says 'that'll do'. Phil has to basically call them off it's that ferocious. That's because they believe in what Phil's doing and that you play how you practise, that's our catch-cry. Play how you practise and you go out there and eat people up. And that's great, because I'm learning to do the same thing. ○

chapter 07

elvis is in the building

Being around Michael can have its perks and despite the frequent crush, one of the nice things is the road can be a lot smoother for you. And I mean that in a literal sense. Sometimes we'll get home from a gruelling road trip and touch down at Chicago airport at two or three in the morning. Michael is always first off the plane, and someone has his car idling in our private lot. He and Scottie have that luxury. I guess they radio ahead when we're coming in. It's often cold and they want their wheels warmed up, ready to fire.

Occasionally, the police block off the traffic exiting the airport so we have a clean, crisp getaway. And Michael's always on the road first in a Ferrari, hot rod Corvette, turbo Porsche, big V12 Mercedes or whatever and he's gone. He basically sweeps the freeway for us. The police turn a blind eye, it's three in the morning, they know we're coming, they know the routine.

Michael likes to drive hard

and he's gone. So it's sort of a game of chasey on the empty freeway heading north. Get your bags, get to your car and go, try to catch him. I never have yet.

Ron Harper is usually in there too, he's got one of everything, he earns good money, about $5 million. He's got a couple of Porsches, a Mercedes, BMW, all kinds of stuff. And then there's Bill. He drives a big

LUC LONGLEY

All work and no play.

campervan. He tries to stay in touch, but it's best to keep out of his way because he hasn't got the speed and therefore uses his girth in a bid to block out those behind. Everyone tries to get out of there before Bill and frankly, it's not that hard. It's a good 25-minute adrenalin rush. It's one of the fun ways to shed the intensity of playing. It's a fringe—albeit mindless—perk of the NBA.

But Michael doesn't always have a burning desire for speed. He can throw a curve ball at ya any time and last season in Texas, he wasn't going to let the warm weather go to waste. We were in San Antonio in November and Michael always travels with five or six body guards, a lot of them older gentlemen, they've been on the Chicago PD a long time, well respected guys. The team though only ever sees them in their suits and working gear.

Well this day we're going to shootaround at the Alamodome, it's a beautiful day in San Antonio. Where's Michael? He's not on the bus. He's decided to ride a push bike to practice. He rented a bunch of those beachcomber bikes and there are three of these old blokes, beer bellies hanging over the beltlines, out in front, wearing shorts, Hawaiian shirts and sunglasses. They were in an arrow shape out front, sort of like a presidential motorcade.

There were three more behind him and one of them wasn't in such good shape as the others and was starting to lag behind. There's Michael, so often shielding himself from the day-to-day swarm of the fan frenzy, zig-zagging his way through mid-morning traffic. It was quite a crack-up to see MJ leading his merry men on a push bike ride to the Alamodome.

My relationship with Michael has developed in to quite a strong one, one based on professional respect. Michael's not the kind of guy you

RUNNING WITH THE BULLS

An excellent point.

LUC LONGLEY

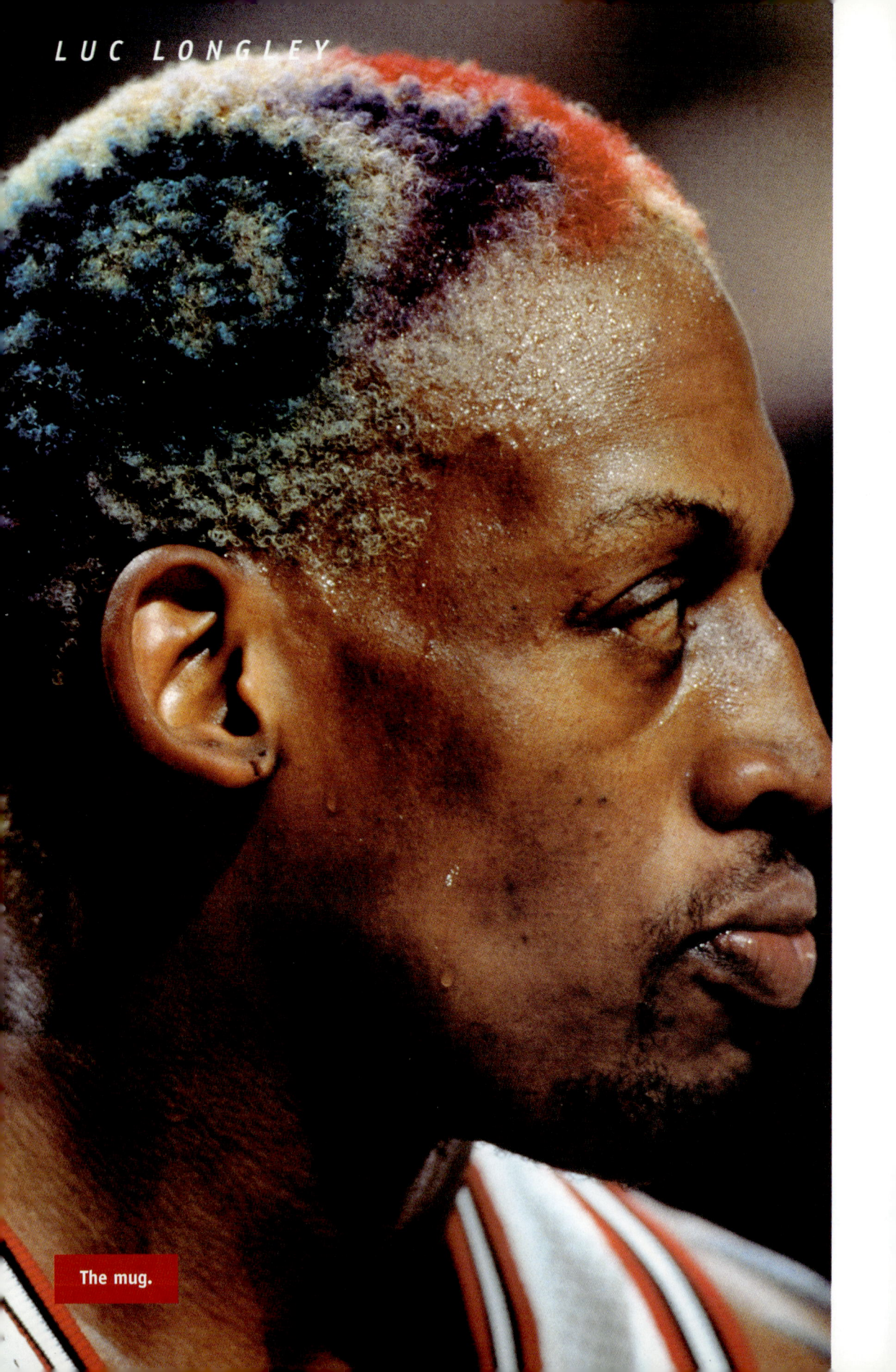

The mug.

RUNNING WITH THE BULLS

What time is it?...Game Time!

Beauty and the Beast.

LUC LONGLEY

Up there Cazaly.

hang out with after a game or at least I certainly don't. Most discussions we have revolve around basketball, but it's very light. Those conversations are frequent, it's the foundation of our relationship.

When you live in each other's pockets for 10 months of the year, the most important thing is to give each other room, especially with Michael. Otherwise you start pissing each other off. One of the great things about the team this year was everyone respected each other enough to give them space, no-one got pushy, the roles were very clear and so there wasn't much jostling for pecking order.

Things that can be a bummer within other teams were non-factors with us and my relationship with Michael was in harmony with that. We had a few good discussions on buses and planes where we'd in fact discuss things other than basketball. I remember asking where he could go now for some privacy. I joked with him he could have gone to Australia two years ago but now that he's playing with me, his profile had been elevated ... he got a chuckle out of that.

The key with Michael was showing him that you care,

but also that you're prepared to do things like play with injuries, do the hard stuff, work hard every day at practice and be as dedicated as he is.

Once he sees that, you've made progress with him for sure. Michael lives in a world that doesn't have much room for a whole bunch of things, it's a pretty full existence. Therefore my feeling has been 'Give him plenty of room.' Don't crowd him and let him be. I think he's thankful for that, the guys on the team don't demand anything from Michael.

Still, I wouldn't swap my lifestyle with him for anything. I think I have the best of both worlds, a little bit of fame, little bit of notoriety, but it's not the Elvis situation that he has.

It's interesting for me. When I'm out, I feel like I'm the centre of attention and everyone wants a piece and I can't give enough, in the last couple of years anyway. I end up begrudging those people who ask me for things because I'm always the focus. As far as I'm concerned I need to respect his space.

A couple of family members and a bunch of friends have sent things in and asked to get Michael to sign them and I resent that. No-one on the team asks anyone else to sign stuff, it's an unwritten code. Early in the year I didn't know how to say no to those people, but it got easier by the end, I got a lot of practice. I could have asked and I'm sure

Mike would have signed the stuff. But I don't want all my teammates bringing me a whole bunch of shit to do either. I've got more than enough to handle with my much lower profile and own bag of tricks, so I can only imagine what his life is like.

He's got enough on his plate, so we make it a sanctuary for him. And because it is a sanctuary, because we're a group of guys he lives with and trusts, he digs every one of us. There's not one of us he wouldn't go in to bat for. Now and again he gets frustrated and yells at one of us, as we do with other players. Sometimes it boils over and it's not surprising there were fights last season. In some ways it's healthy. He and Steve Kerr got into a full-on rumble in the first month of training camp in October 1995.

MJ packs a punch most middle weights would die for.

There was a lot pressure on him at camp, he thought people were saying he wasn't the same player, and that he'd aged. And so he was obsessed with perfection and domination, traits that took him to greatness before his retirement. Every possession down the floor he wanted to shoot the ball, every game was life and death for him, he was going nuts. Camps are long and we were getting sick of it after a while. MJ was out of control. He was on a mission.

MJ was talking shit at practice and Steve was on the opposing team having to guard him. Michael was dominating, shooting not passing, taunting Steve, declaring 'No-one could do anything' against him. Steve went to drive by him and lowered his shoulder in to Mike, drawing the contact. Mike probably fouled him, but it was MJ who was snarling like a junkyard dog. He glared down at Steve and barked 'I'm not BJ (Armstrong, former teammate)!' It was like 'Who do you think you're messing with, boy?'

So on the next play Steve went down the lane and MJ gave him a forearm shiver, so Steve gave him the same back on the next play and it was on. If it was ice hockey, Mike would have had the gloves off and been in to Steve before the gloves hit the ground. Mike was incensed and was just giving it to Steve. It was like a Grizzly taking a swipe at a Koala. The biffo lasted all of 10 seconds, but worked its way from under the basket to the baseline wall about 15 feet away before the boys jumped in.

As we peeled Mike off, Steve was already showing signs of a black eye. It developed into a serious shiner. MJ was so pissed off about it all, he just walked out of practice. That's how intense the practices were.

MJ called Steve later that night and apologised and it was accepted by Steve, who had earned a lot of respect out of the incident. Talking to Steve about that later, in many ways it was good because those things break the ice, they break down the barriers between a guy like MJ and Steve. Like me, Steve had only played with MJ at the end of the 1995 season when he came back after retirement. We all had to learn to understand each other, and for us it was a lesson in how he was driven by the pressure and the expectation.

Michael doesn't always get away scot free, and he's like anybody, he doesn't want to be yelled at. But you can go into a timeout and say 'This is what's happening' and you can talk to him, he's quite prepared to change what he's doing, or admit he was wrong. He respects us that much. But he's a very proud man, I don't think anyone yelled at him this year. There's always a lot of shit talking at practice where we tell each other to 'Piss off', or 'You're not going to block this' and that sort of stuff. But there's been no reason to yell at him. The closest I've come to yelling at him is in retaliation to when he's got under my skin and I thought it was over the top.

In that case, rather than make a big scene of it, I'm more the kind of bloke that's going to go to him afterwards and say, 'Hey Mike, I'd appreciate if you wouldn't do that.' Through the course of the year he got to understand the way I did things. I think early on, he considered my reluctance to yell at people and get combative as a sign of weakness. But I honestly believe by the end of the year, he realised it was a sign of strength.

That's why I was consistent for us through the season. I didn't waver through emotional ups and downs. I was just steady and that's what they needed from me, and Mike was mindful of that.

We're cool now and our relationship is as strong as anyone's on the team, but I'd have to say after he came back, I really didn't like the guy. I found him difficult to be around and he and I obviously didn't see eye to eye. We were at each other's throats in practice and as I said before, that was a case of frustration from both of us, mostly from him.

But we got over it early this year, right away, and we both made a point, or I did certainly, of recognising that if it was going to work, we had to figure out what was happening. It was mostly basketball stuff. Once we figured out how to play together, it was cool.

He figured that out over summer and came into camp last season looking for the things I could do and using and appreciating those, instead of looking for my faults. I have faults, my game's not the full package, there are things that are limited. I'm not a great rebounder and I can't catch the ball on the move in traffic and finish at the rim. He recognised that and now he doesn't give me the ball in traffic any-

LUC LONGLEY

Mr Clean.

more. That's when he came out with the line if I 'didn't start catching his passes he'd throw it right at my head'. I was coming through the lane for a rebounding position, it was within the first couple of days of his return and he hit me with the ball. I just don't have the legs and feet to handle that situation.

That's why I came back to Chicago after the surgery the summer following the championship, so I could develop the leg strength which would enable me to change my momentum at the last second. But I'm a big heavy guy, a bit like a runaway freight train. Once I get going in one direction, it's not always easy to change tracks.

I think you'll find he'll be one of my biggest endorsers and was most of last season, too. He knows I can help his game and the team's. Defensively, I'm always backing him. Offensively, I'm setting big picks for him, screening him free, trying to protect him from other big guys in altercations, although he'd rather handle it himself to tell you the truth. He likes that stuff, it gets him fired up.

He realises the fact that I'm a competent scorer. I give him an outlet, especially on a screen and roll. I flare out for that 15-foot jump shot and he loves to hit me with that pass because I shoot it at a pretty good clip. Michael knows if I get the ball in the post and he uses a rub screen or a baseline cut, he'll get the ball back in the right rhythm to shoot the ball. He knows he can make back cuts when he's being overplayed and I'll bounce the ball down low for him. He goes to the hole because that's one of the things I bring to this team, passing.

In the Finals, Seattle did a better job than most of covering up the backdoor cut, that's one of our key pressure release plays if we can't get the ball into our sideline entry. I'd flash high post, they'd hit me with the ball and Michael would be one of the wings and would cut backdoor having been overplayed. That was our bread and butter all year. Teams would try to put the pressure on us in the third and fourth quarter, we'd get a couple of those plays and break their backs. Those kind of basketball things were the cornerstone of our relationship.

ELVIS IS IN THE BUILDING

To know and play with Michael is really something,

he's an incredible individual. He won't accept losing, won't accept thinking anybody's got the better of him, in any situation. Messing around with him in the locker room, he likes to come out on top, whether it's cards, golf, ping pong, yahtzee, whatever. I care about basketball but I'm not ultra competitive, though my brothers might tell you differently. So I won't step into a lot of his competitive environments because they don't interest me. But that's where he lives. He knows that I'll back him up on court but he'd like to think he doesn't need it and didn't all year.

There's a multitude of things that make us different and perhaps a lot of it stems from our respective backgrounds. He's just a very intense, competitive, aggressive person that goes straight at any goal with a supreme self confidence that borders on arrogance. I tend to be a little too selfless at times. I get the job done in a manner I feel comfortable with. I wouldn't be on this team if Michael didn't like me or didn't like what I was doing. I don't think he controls the team, but if he didn't like me I wouldn't be around. He has that power, he's that strong a personality.

His return improved all of us, I hesitate to say he took my game to

Contrast in styles, leaving our Orlando villas.

57

LUC LONGLEY

58   Two high flying Bulls practise before the game.

another level because he tends to get credit for a lot of things, including other people's hard work. But he brought an intensity level, a practice focus I thought we already had, yet Michael simply lifted it to another degree. Through practice or games, Michael's complete professionalism rubbed off on the team and took everything to a higher plane. The kind of work ethic and practice intensity that I've adopted over the last couple of years, is what has elevated my game. You could attribute some of it to him, and yes, he's certainly been the leading light.

One of the amazing things about Michael is his presentation, clean is the word the guys like to use. Always fresh pressed shirt, ties, matching suit, shoes, the whole package. He's corporate America, put together with clinical precision. In many cases, one of his several different coloured Ferraris will match the colour of his suit. He also has three different coloured 850 BMWs, although you don't see those around much anymore, he's into Ferraris, they are his pets. That's what you get I guess with his sort of disposable income.

Obviously he and Nike are pretty tight, I don't think I've seen him in the same Nike gear twice, ever. And it's always something you've never seen before. People know he wears a new pair of shoes every night, but sometimes it's two pairs. He'll warm up in a pair and put on a fresh pair before tip-off. He's got four pairs in his bag before each game and if he's playing badly, he might come in and change them, you never know. I think he puts all that stuff to good use, passing it on to charity auctions and the gear to friends and family. He has a foundation he does a lot of stuff with, Michael certainly does his fair share of charity work, no doubt about that.

He is the undisputed leader of this team. He's said at times it's Scottie's team but that's rubbish. It's Phil's team and it's Michael's team. Phil is obviously the leader, no doubt, he works closely with Michael and as far as the players are concerned it's his baby, that's the way it is.

MJ deserves so much respect and you see it in the way he performs every night. When we needed a clutch basket, every time it was a close game, Michael would end up taking the shot and usually make it. I remember in Vancouver we were playing terribly and I was awful. It was our first major road trip west. Three nights earlier we'd lost to Seattle 97–92 where I had my career high 21 points. Michael had the ball stolen by Gary Payton in the closing seconds to seal the win. The following night, MJ had a crucial steal to clinch a 107–104 win over Portland. In Vancouver we were struggling again and were down by 12 to the Grizzlies with something like three minutes to play and Michael just put on a display as if to say, 'Enough is enough. This is not right, we're losing to an expansion team.'

Byron Scott was trying to guard him and he'd blow by Scott which wasn't that hard, but what was impressive was getting to the ring, changing his shot two or three times, drifting by a couple of defenders, and flipping the ball up on the other side of the rim. He didn't do it once, he scored something like our last 15 points, he would take the ball and basically say 'Get out of the way and enjoy the show.' I hope he was talking trash because that was one of the times he should have been. He had 19 points in the final six minutes. And at the other end, he was getting steals and grabbing boards, he just took over the game like I've never seen before.

I think

he's the best trash talker in the league

because he can back it up. I think trash talk only makes you look bad if you don't back it up and that's partly why I don't do it. He's the master yapper because he'll tell you what he's going to do to you, and then look at you and say 'Okay next.' Payton made the mistake in the Finals of continuing to talk and while Gary did a reasonable job, I think Michael more than got his point across.

I usually can't hear it, I'm doing my own thing and he's often in another part of the court anyway. Certainly you realise when he's made a big shot or something's happened, you make a point to look in that direction and he's always up to something. He's the ultimate competitor and showman, he recognises the value in that. I don't think it's a con job, you're seeing the real deal. You're seeing the make-up of his personality shining through.

An interesting illustration of MJ's ability to play the whole game and do whatever was required was when Dennis got kicked out at New Jersey for the head-butt. We were down in the first half and he hauled in 16 rebounds in Dennis's absence. It was another demonstration of his will to win. Mike had 37 points and we got up 97–93. It was also his sixth of eight straight games where he had 30 or more points, all of them wins.

Sometimes you do tend to sit back and enjoy the show, like his little encore performance at Vancouver. At Philadelphia, one of MJ's former alumni Jerry Stackhouse, a rookie with the 76ers, made the foolish mistake of stating the NBA wasn't as hard as he envisaged and declared nobody could stop him. Michael lit him up for 48 in our 120–93 cruise just to let him know the game could be a chore to those who didn't continually work hard.

A month later, the Pistons took us to OT before we got up at their place 112–109. Detroit was feeling good about themselves when they

ELVIS IS IN THE BUILDING

That's why they call him Superman.

arrived at the United Center for the return bout in March. They were on a pretty good winning streak at the time and securing a play-off berth. Doug Collins, the Pistons coach, was also Mike's first coach at the Bulls and so it was a bit of a home-coming for Collins, who had spent some time as a broadcaster on TNT. The Pistons had co-rookie of the year Grant Hill and were a good young team. I think Michael recognises the potential heirs to his throne and puts heavy emphasis on keeping them in their place. It's his court and he's still the king.

Michael had the quietest 53 points I've ever seen on Detroit that night and we crushed them 102–81. The thing about Michael is he scores so easily. You can't tell the difference between 30 and 50 with Michael. I've looked up and thought, 'Wow he must have a lot of points' and he's only got 30. That night it didn't even occur to me that it was out of the norm and he had 53, an NBA season high last year. Just to rub it in, he had 30 in late April as we blew the Pistons out at home in the third last game of the season, 110–79.

But Mike's not so proud he won't recognise talent. He and Scottie love the Wolves' Kevin Garnett, they think he's the next big thing. But

MJ takes pride in recognising talent and then measuring himself against it.

He'll look at a guy and think 'Shit he's good. If I can go out and crush him, then I'm still the man.' You see that night after night in Mike.

He's got no mercy. If someone's down, he'll kick them in the guts. At practice, and especially at camp, he loves to get those young, fresh faced hopefuls that come in who are intimidated by him. They aren't really sure how to handle him, but they end up guarding him, and as far as Michael's concerned, that's high hilarity, he muses 'How bad can I make this guy look?' But he makes great NBA players look bad too. It is interesting, though, to see these young guys that come in and have nothing to lose, sneak one in on him now and then.

With eight scoring titles, Michael is well versed at putting the ball in the hole and winning games, just ask Craig Ehlo. But the unbelievable thing about Michael is that he plays both ends of the court, he can dominate a game defensively, as much as he can dominate a game offensively.

We call him the 'Black Cat' because it's like having a panther on your side.

He prowls quietly, sizing up his prey, creeps low to the ground and is ready to pounce at any moment.

He's so quick, teams have to spread their passing angles out an extra 20–30 degrees because he can get out in the lane with blinding speed. If you have the ball, you want to pick that sucker up and pass it. He's all over it like a cat on a mouse. He toys with people defensively, forces them into mistakes, forces them in to areas where they are going to take a bad shot. A lot of times he forces them into me. I had a career high seven blocks against Milwaukee last year and Mike was right, they kept shooting into my hands. They were just trying to get away from Mike and avoid embarrassment. That's where I stepped in.

If he's out gambling on the passing lane and gets back cut, I'm the one who has to step up in to the hole and take care of traffic, take a hard foul now and again. That's why I had a bit of foul trouble last year, but I'm happy with the role, and maybe Michael wouldn't be doing that if he knew I wasn't there backing him up.

Nobody on the Bulls was scared to fail, or relent and say 'We'll give them that.' We didn't give anyone anything. Ever. That's what made us a great defensive team and Scottie, Michael and Dennis are three of the best in the business. The whole Michael Jordan thing is a blast, that's for sure. Now and then we're on the sideline and we're discussing, or arguing about a play, drawing up stuff and I sit back and think 'This is really cool. I'm doing this with the best there is.'

chapter 8

the bank's open

Two summers ago I had to make a few decisions on money, contracts and future interests. The vexing question to me when I came out of contract with the Bulls in June 1995, which finished my first four-year deal in the NBA, was to sign for one season, or take in the security of a longer term deal, and perhaps not make as much money.

Who was to know a year later the insane money NBA owners would be willing to spend on players, and some very ordinary players at that. I loved the Bulls and many of us, including myself, were already looking ahead to 1995–96 after our inglorious exit from the play-offs at the hands of Orlando.

I knew Michael would be coming out of contract in 12 months time (June 1996) and that was going to be an expensive exercise for the Bulls' management. I decided to take a firm offer sheet from the Bulls that would pay me an average

$3m a year over the next three years.

I didn't want to be left in the lurch a year later, should the Bulls have to dump free agents off the roster in order to keep Jordan and attract other talent. I could sense a championship was near. I went with security first and it was a good move. Later we signed Dennis and he too had one year left on his contract.

Normal payment method for NBA players is every two weeks over a six-month period, or pretty much the duration of the NBA season. That's a whopping pay cheque every fortnight, let me tell you. However, this year (and I believe Michael and I are the only two Bulls players to have this in our contracts) I got paid the entire year's pay on November 1st. It makes a lot of sense. For someone like me, that can be as much as $75,000 interest after taxes have been taken out. Why have someone else make money out of my salary when I can?

Considering where I started, living in a dorm room as a spindly teen at the AIS and then a partially subsidised (by my father) life at college, living on $335 a month with a $200 a month apartment rental, I've come a long way for sure. I toiled hard like any other struggling college student, I had a very economical car and ate a lot of rice. It was only in my last two years at the University of New Mexico that I recognised the NBA was a realistic objective, an objective that would come with all the trappings of a fat salary. But I had never understood the worth of money, and how little it was worth. I thought I could do everything with a million dollars, but I learned quickly.

I'd certainly never encountered tax as an issue either and suddenly I'm writing a $750,000 tax cheque from my first year's income, which was $US1.6m. It suddenly occurred to me 'Hey, tax means they take your money.' I had never paid a cent of tax before in my life, because I'd never worked, this was my first real job. Signing my name on that cheque as a 22-year-old professional basketballer was a big-time reality check for me.

It's funny that although they pay us vast sums of money, clubs remain inclined to give us $100 a day on road trips. Basically it's meal money, which is tax deductable. And we eat every cent of it too, because they put us in the most expensive hotels they can find. Though I know some of the guys on minimum wage try to save some of it. A 12-day road trip can add up.

We've always been given meal money, it's part of the league. We also get a full dental and health plan, a retirement fund we get access to after 10 years in the league, like a pension. There's a superannuation fund of sorts too. We get looked after when our playing days are over.

There are plenty of perks in this lifestyle,

but mostly because people just seem to want to do a lot for a professional sportsman. They want to be associated with you, help you out, get you into places like the theatre, restaurants, give you an extra big feed. Over the summer, I did a deal with the local Chicago Jeep dealer.

In exchange for two tickets to every Chicago regular season home game, which I bought for him, I received (for one year only) a 1997 Limited Edition Jeep Cherokee with everything on it, so our nanny could have a car to get around in with the kids.

I needed another vehicle, because I'd just given the old Bronco (and nanny car) to an old friend from Albuquerque who'd helped me rebuild it. So the Jeep was a nice perk, but perks are getting harder to come by. A couple of years ago you could have got them tickets to every second game. The dealerships are getting greedy.

I guess one other thing I'm going to treat myself to is a Harley Davidson. I figure I'll buy one for every championship we win, that's my own private trophy. I'll save it for the back roads of Western Australia since Chicago roads are a bit wild. I hope it will be understated, almost quietly a Bulls championship bike in that it will have that engraved on it somewhere. I had it in the works for some time and as the year wore on it became more apparent it would be a good idea.

It's 14 inches longer than a regular bike and it's being built by Arlen Ness, who's the guru of custom motorcycles from California. If you're getting a Harley, you get Arlen to build it.

The most glaring reminder to measure my income and its relative value against, is my father, who's worked really hard all his life, 18 hours a day sometimes. He's got his own architecture practice, he started it in his backroom so he could be around the kids when we grew up. He's built it up and it's been a struggle for him, with Australia's economic situation architecture is a tough profession to be in. And to watch all the work he's done and to realise that within my first couple of years of my professional life, I was already ahead in terms of net income.

Dad told me when he got his first pay cheque from his first job, his first real job, he went out and spent it all on oysters and champagne, because he felt that was an appropriate thing to do. Of course my first cheque from my first job was a million bucks. You'd be pretty sick on oysters and champagne. I bought a property down in the southwest of WA, bought my mother a car, helped my brothers out with some land, a bunch of other stuff, spent a lot of it. I paid off my Bronco and bought Kelly a car.

When we were in Minnesota that was one of my more romantic moments. I bought her a Carrera 4 convertible, with all the right gear on it. I picked her up for dinner and surprised her by throwing her the keys. She was blown away, just giggled for a minute in astonishment. I made a point of booking a restaurant about 45 minutes out of town so she could take it for a spin. She giggled the whole way there. She loves it and longs for summer so she can get it out of the garage. Those

LUC LONGLEY

Our new place is home to more than the Longleys.

are the kind of ridiculous things you are able to do which are a bit bizarre.

Some say I have a big fleet of cars, but not compared to other guys. Michael is an extreme example, but Ronnie and Toni like their cars also. I guess cars are a bit of a thing for me, I love cars, always have, and used to race a little Honda CRX back in Albuquerque, which was great fun. Even more fun was watching me squeeze my way into it, it was a bit like forcing a banana into a matchbox.

Cars are perhaps my biggest tangible perk. It's not like I walk around in Armani suits, I don't wear a lot of jewellery, don't have expensive art. I've just bought a new house, but it's not over the top, just a bit bigger. We were running out of room with two young children and a full-time nanny.

When the average salary is over $1m and guys like myself, who are role players and not stars in the league by any stretch, are making $3–4 million, it's insane. For example, Jim McIlvaine, another seven footer who averaged under three points and three rebounds last season at Washington, is a guy I believe has had an inferior career to me. He's certainly a good player, but I think I have more to offer and he just signed a seven-year, $US35 million contract with Seattle. When guys like him and myself are making $3 and $5 million, the money's ludicrous.

But it's also a reflection of the state of the league. How many Bulls hats, how much NBA paraphernalia do kids wear on the street? It's a completely fashionable industry. In the new collective bargaining agreement they included merchandise, so what we had been getting in the past didn't include the merchandise and that's a billion-dollar-a-year industry worldwide.

Last season was the first of the new collective bargaining agreement and we finally received a decent cut of the merchandise. Every player got $70,000 last year from merchandise, $35,000 after tax, which is a vast improvement on the past. I'll sign a new deal with Nike this year close to $50,000 a season and our play-off bonuses from the league last year were roughly $160,000 each.

The NBA owners and the league are killing the pig. The league is healthy, we're making salaries that befit the industry we're providing entertainment for. While we're earning ridiculous salaries, I don't think we're ripping anyone off either. The games are accessible, people enjoy it, it's a spectacular sport and kids are into it. It's a fashion statement for kids right now.

But the real perks aren't the cars, houses, first class travel and stuff like that, that's materialistic. The real perk is time. I can buy time, I can hire people to help take care of mundane chores that keep people from their families. I can then afford the time to take my kids to the pool, whatever, just be around them more and watch them grow up.

People ask me what I do outside of basketball, that's easy. My family is where the rest of my time goes. I spend as much of my non-basketball time as possible just hanging out with them. I spend a lot of time with Clare and Lily. We have a cleaning lady 2-3 times a week and a nanny who helps Kelly with the kids while I'm on the road.

Clare is one of my greatest motivations.

Money aside though, it's a positive existence being in a winning environment like the Chicago Bulls. The coaching staff handed me an incredible opportunity here to play and I've been rewarding them. I would have had my family and my daughters regardless of where I played. But if I was miserable in Minnesota, I don't think I'd have the energy to enjoy them as much as I do now.

Above all else, the number one thing the salary is affording me is to be able to set myself up later in life to have a choice to do what I want to do, regardless of making money. Hopefully, if I'm smart about it, I'll do the things that interest me. I don't know what they are just yet, but I'll figure them out.

And the girls will be taken care of. They will have a certain degree of financial security for the rest of their lives as well.

That's my aim, to set my family up

so when I'm finished hoopin', finished banging heads with Shaq and Patrick, they are still going to be young children that I can be around. I can afford to give them a father who is there a lot for them and that's what I'm looking forward to. I certainly want my kids to grow up in Australia, I can't think of anywhere more ideal.

Take a look at Michael and he's on every billboard, every TV station, every radio ad endorsing products, mostly Nike, Oakley, Wheaties (I'm actually on a cereal box with him this year), Wilson balls and recently Renew batteries. It's worth astronomical money to him, over $54m a year. But I'm different, I haven't embraced a lot of commercial activity in the past because my time is more valuable to me than trying to make more money selling products. However, there seem to be so many opportunities this year, I felt it was a good chance to give something back to the kids and the community.

So what I've done is create a foundation where I'll be doing a lot more commercial ventures, including this book, and all my royalties will go to people a lot less fortunate than I am. Hopefully that will be a sizeable amount. I'm proud of the foundation and I think it's a worthwhile initiative, I feel it offsets my feeling of being spoiled.

And here are the other two.

And I do feel pretty spoiled at times, but what are you going to do if you are making that kind of money, give it all away? No. I've looked after the family, taken care of people that needed a hand. But obviously I feel as though I'm one of the lucky ones. Now it's time to put a smile on the faces of some kids who aren't. ○

chapter 9

on the road with the beatles

Spend a road trip with the Bulls and you'd soon get a handle on the circus that follows. It is out of control, and you'll never believe some of the lengths the team must go to just to get around without causing traffic jams and mass hysteria among fans. You can thank Michael for most of that, but the acquisition of Dennis and the already substantial popularity of Scottie went a long way to contributing to the incessant crush of human interest. I like the fans and will sign autographs and have pictures taken when I can, but constantly dealing with the people can wear you out.

You tend to get a lot of lobby traffic in the hotels, people just hanging out wanting something. They want a piece of you, they've got something in mind for you, business propositions, people who want to be your agent, people who want you to do a camp, who want you to sign things, people who want you go to a bar mitzvah, people asking for shoes, uniforms, people who want to eat with you, dads saying 'This is my kid, he's a big fan, can we have breakfast or lunch?'

In some cases people are even claiming to be long lost family. There's a lot of long lost family in the NBA, distant cousins in need. People are always coming up to me saying 'Hey man, I'm Michael's cousin, Scottie's cousin, what room's he in?' I say 'Michael who?' or 'He's in another hotel.'

Away from the responsibility of the kids, the road can make game preparation easier in many respects and I can relax in my room, do my own thing in my own time. But in terms of getting around and doing things, the road's a drain because if it's the first or second time we've been to a particular town then everybody's out to catch us. We have our own plane, so the travel doesn't wear me out as much as the aggressive energy of the people in other cities.

It's good I have friends in a lot of towns now. I can meet them to get out of the vicinity of the hotel. Then you can go to a pub and it's not so bad. Walk out of the hotel in a big city and people are on you, making more contact than Shaq in the post.

Last year in New York during the play-offs, I walked out of the Plaza, a plush midtown hotel that sits across the street from Central Park, and there were 15 television cameras from all around the world. Probably 300 people crammed around the front entrance of the hotel, it was packed. And they're all there to see the Bulls. As soon as I walked out, the flashes were blinding, pens whizzed out of pockets, autograph books were thrust in my face, and the long lost cousins showed up again. It was different this year to days gone by, the Beatles factor was in full swing because of Michael.

A Big Apple throng.

I'm a starter on the Bulls championship team, yet I can walk outside at least and get a cab, go downtown in NY and grab a feed. With that crush outside, MJ, Scottie and Dennis just wouldn't be able to do it. It would be a nightmare. It's because of those distractions that the Bulls' organisation makes it easier for us, in many ways they have to.

We've got our own charter jet, it used to be an MGM executive plane. Private planes used to be a luxury for many NBA teams, now they are a necessity. When we drive to Chicago airport, we park at a private lot right next to the tarmac and take a bus right out to the steps to the plane, jump on and the plane is gone.

To have to walk through an airport, sit in a lounge and wait to board, like regular passengers, would potentially shut the airport down because pilots, flight attendants, baggage handlers, ground staff, you name it, would simply stop. On domestic, non-basketball flights, I've had staff from airport restaurants or whatever, just drop their duties and race out for autographs.

That's one of the conveniences of charter, you don't have to use the terminal, it's a facility for people like us. But in my first year in Minnesota, we flew commercial and even with the lowly Timberwolves, who had no real high-profile athletes, it was a big deal at the gate and getting on the plane with parents and their kids tugging at our shirt tails.

So it's nice to have it like it is. You couldn't do it any other way with Michael and Scottie and Dennis, it would just be a circus. So we walk across the tarmac and jump on the plane. It's a league rule that teams must fly out to the game the night before. The only way you can get in that morning is if you have back-to-back games in different cities. So if we played in Chicago tonight, after the game we'd all drive out to the airport, jump on the plane and fly into the next snow covered town.

Champions fly Champion Air.

The MGM jet is luxurious. It's got leather couches, a bar, some booths at the back with TV monitors for watching game film, the coaches are usually back there. It's First Class travel without paying a cent. We've got a smorgasbord chock full of healthy food. Normal Bulls fare while airborne is pasta and chicken, something like that. It's certainly better than regular plane food, but I still usually don't eat it to tell you the truth, I usually wait until the hotel.

General manager Jerry Krause travels with us quite often and we take a few of the Bulls media guys with us, not the beat writers from the dailies who take delight in ripping us every other day, but more the Bulls' employed media, our broadcasters and so on.

I sit by myself, I have a couple of chairs up the front. Michael has a cabin, like a train booth down the back where he and Scottie, Randy and Ron play cards.

Dennis can liven things up for the boys on those long trans-continental flights.

He put some pornography on the overhead screens one night and the female flight attendants weren't too happy about that. Phil came up to the front of the plane and turned it off, which, as you can imagine, was a bit of a shame for the boys. Dennis got in the habit of bringing videos for each flight. He was in charge of in-flight entertainment being the most single guy with the most time on his hands and the

LUC LONGLEY

Dennis is the pilot of his own ship.

most bored.

NBA expansion has added a new and interesting dimension to travel with two teams now in Canada—Vancouver and Toronto. Customs is more relaxed than Athens, Greece, with no bag checks, passport verification or sniffer dogs. So far it has just been two to three agents coming through the plane asking for autographs. It's a real captive audience, you know, they get a chance to meet the Bulls.

When we're on the road it's a novelty for so many people. Often we get bad service just because people are trippin', people are into it, people are looking to rub shoulders. Consequently, a lot of the guys—I haven't had to do it until fairly recently—use an alias. I can't tell you our aliases because they're aliases.

Obviously Michael uses an alias. Quite often, depending on the road trip, he'll travel with five, six, seven security guards. Certainly when he's in Chicago, if he's going out he's always got two or three with him at least. As I understand it, they have hotel rooms around his, on either side and across the hall, to keep him tucked away because Michael draws an awful lot of attention, he's like a rock star. I don't need to tell you that. We actually dubbed him Elvis. 'He's in the building'.

Basically he and Scottie ask for suites. They pay the extra and they get the big luxury suite. In actual fact, in the NBA you're supposed to have roommates but no-one wants one, so you automatically get the cost of having a single room as opposed to a double deducted from your paycheque. If you're smart and there's 13 guys travelling, you say 'I want a roommate because I don't want a deduction' and obviously no-one will room with you because no-one wants a roommate. You end up getting someone else to pay for your room. In five years I've never had a roommate yet.

When we stay in five star hotels, Ritz Carltons, Four Seasons, in some cities, we drive the bus down in to the back of the hotel, walk up through the kitchen, up the service elevators and in through the laundry—that's kind of cool.

The best one is the Ritz Carlton at Pentagon City. During the day, when people aren't waiting for you to arrive or waiting for you to go to the game, we'll simply walk out and do our thing. That particular hotel in Washington is adjoined to a mall, so we go down and get a feed and it's not too bad.

The trick is to keep moving and sit down quick.

But Michael wouldn't really go to a mall that much, he wouldn't be able to and Scottie probably wouldn't. I can get away with it, same with Steve, Jud and Toni, although Toni's got a lot of star power and it's harder for him. People love him, you know, he's got quite a high profile. He gets a lot of television, a lot of highlight reel type of stuff. As they say, he's supposed to be the next great one.

This year it was as if the Bulls gave some mystical meaning to a mundane regular season and each city we went to was an asterisk on the calendar for thousands of opposing fans. In Phoenix, MJ caused two hysterical females to faint when they got close enough to touch him. In Denver, it was well below freezing and we finally arrived at the hotel around 4am but there was a lobby loaded with autograph hounds. At Miami, a group of Japanese tourists jumped to attention when they recognised Michael. And there are always fans, mostly girls, hovering around hotels trying to catch a glimpse of any of us, some will even try to book rooms in the hotels in a bid to get closer.

Basically fans love us everywhere. It's probably a lot to do with Michael's marketing power and our winning brand of basketball. We sold out everywhere, even in venues like Atlanta, where the Hawks struggle for large crowds, we were getting more applause than the home club. Same in Miami and that got Alonzo Mourning pretty pissed off. 'I got sick to my stomach when I heard that,' Zo told local media. He said 'They cheered louder for them than they did for us and we're the home team, that's ridiculous.'

Dennis is right when he calls us a three-ring circus, and he's one of the three rings. How about New York, where the weird and the wonderful can share the same seat on the bus? One road game there, we were staying at the Plaza as usual and Michael had planned a meeting and therefore some businessmen decked out in three-piece pin striped suits mingled in the lobby below some expensive art. Right next to them, a group of tattoo-decorated cross-dressing men and women waited patiently for Dennis. The juxtaposition was hilarious.

I don't see much of MJ on the road. NBA guys don't hang a lot together. Teams don't eat together, there's no arranged pre-game meal, no after match function like in the NBL. It's every man for himself, just be on the bus at the prescribed time to get to the game. From what I can gather, Michael has his entourage and pretty much stays in his room. If he does go out, he's got a discreet side entrance with a car waiting and BOOM, he's gone to somewhere that's expecting him and they just shuffle him right in and keep the security guards around him. So it's all a question of management for Michael.

A lot of times we'll get to a city the night before we play and there'll be a couple of limos out the front. Usually for a Dennis, a Scottie or a Michael, those guys have to travel that way, really. They've gotten to a point where it's not like they can wait on a street corner for a cab. I can get away with it more, although when I was in Atlanta for the Games it was necessary for me to get a limo for the four days, because I was staying 20 miles out of town and post-NBA championship, I had become a mild celebrity. Everyone knew who I was and it did create an unwanted crowd. To have a car waiting was useful, necessary and convenient.

Leaving the arenas can be interesting too. When we've jumped on the bus to head to the hotel or straight to the airport, we've had people driving alongside the bus at night with torches looking in the window, hanging out of sunroofs trying to see us.

At times, we've had to have police escorts,

where they shut down the traffic and let us straight through. There are always carloads of people, often girls, following the bus, trying to get in through the airport, trying to get on to the tarmac so that they can be there when we get off the bus.

Leaving places like Madison Square Garden in New York, it's just a throng of people, mostly Knicks' fans hating us, loving to hate us. It's interesting to watch people as they recognise us, as they hear the murmur that 'It's the Bulls bus!', they just stop in their tracks and check it out. Every day I realise more and more that the NBA is entertainment, or in the Dennis vernacular, it's theatre.

My typical road trip agenda goes something like this. I pick up Jud, drive to the airport (we'll eat peanut butter and jam sandwiches on the way to home games), jump on the plane as I described, watch a movie, or whatever on the plane. Say we're going to Cleveland, we get a three or four o'clock flight and get in to town at sort of six or seven, check in, and do the regular routine of getting all your bags organised. We never handle our bags, basically the bellman delivers our bags, picks them up from the room, puts them on the bus, the whole bit. So then the boys will go out and I might call my mates in that town to organise a feed, catch a movie or just kill time that night.

If I'm in a party mood I'll hang with Dennis, more often than not I'm hanging with Toni, Jud and Steve. Some people thought Toni was a guy who liked a beer on road trips, but not really. Toni's actually the least likely to drink, which is unusual because he has a reputation—Croatians, Yugoslavians are always known for, sort of, drinking and smoking on the day of the game. So I think he's sort of countered that by really going overboard in the other direction.

Bill's a bit more of a solo bird and does his own thing. Because we play in so many east coast cities and being from the east and going to college at St John's in New York, Bill's got family back there. He's out visiting. Most of us have been in the league long enough that we have regular haunts, we know how to get there, we can give them a call, get a table. There's really nothing flashy about that.

A lot of the guys sleep in until shootaround, which is usually 10-11am on game day. It entails going to the arena on the bus, walking through our scouting reports, Phil makes 40-50 coaching points, defensive rotations, match-ups, how to handle screen and rolls, offensive emphasis, the triangle, sort of tweaking us, tuning us in to the team we're playing. In the play-offs it's even more than that.

Security gets a taste of Bulls mania.

Shootarounds are no party, it's an integral aspect of our preparation and critical to our success. We get a feel for the gym, get used to the background, the depth of the seating, that makes a big difference to shooting. Every rim in the NBA has a different tension, on some backboards the ball slips off them, like it's really slippery, others are very sticky and the ball grabs. You have to get used to how the rim and backboard work together, because they're all different. The United Center for instance is renowned for having slippery backboards and tight rings, we shoot a horrible percentage in the United Center.

The old Boston Garden was a classic. There were literally patches where you wouldn't bounce the ball, where bits of the floor came together, a four corner situation in the parquet jigsaw, where the difference was half an inch in height. One corner was up, one corner was down. It was shocking. You had to know that. The Celtics, as crafty as they were, obviously wanted to trap you in that corner where the ball dies. They'd see people heading towards it, especially young guys who didn't know about it, then run at them, they'd go to pick the ball up and it wouldn't be there, it would still be on the floor.

A lot of these arenas have got their real quirks.

Where are the shot clocks, where are the scoreboards, how does the ball come out of the nets? Teams that like to fast break, a Don Nelson team, the Warriors of old, teams that like to run, they'll have nets that are real loose and stretched out so the ball comes through quickly and you can go with it and ignite the break from out of bounds. They also have balls with more air pressure in them so they bounce long off the glass.

Simple and it makes sense—long rebounds, fast breaks. Phil carries a needle around with him and is constantly letting air out of the balls because we like to have a bit more control, we like a tighter rebound situation and we'll fast break with our energy, rather than the energy of the ball. Those teams that have loose nets and hard balls are Western Conference teams, teams that like to run. Seattle did exactly that.

Phil must be a pain to opposition stadium staff. He will quite often request that new nets be put up, that's part of his thing. You can easily make sure a net gets changed, all you have to do is cut it down. If a team scares him he might ask for a change. If you don't think a team can beat you then you won't worry about it. I don't think Phil does that all the time, but I'm sure he was concerned against Seattle where they can generate so much energy off a long rebound and get the ball out of bounds and go. Whereas we'd almost rather have nets that caught the ball, swung it around for a minute then let it plop out. You see that a lot in the East.

So you have to be tuned in. Because the NBA is so one-on-one, two-on-two orientated, a lot of the time is spent scouting those situations, where double teams are forced, either on the wing, or with a screen and roll. So when we're playing Utah, you know Johnny Stockton and Karl Malone are going to set a screen on the wing 25 times a game.

You have to work out which way you're going to force them. If you're going to double team them, where are you going to double team from. Remember on the back side you're two-on-three, because you've got three-on-two on the ball. Because Stockton's such an efficient passer, you have to make adjustments.

But then Phil will say if it's John Stockton and Felton Spencer (now at Orlando) we'll do it this way. Each of the opposition's half dozen scoring options we break down and walk through. Utah uses a cross screen for Karl Malone on the baseline, then they use a double up screen, two screens up at the foul line, to roll him to the post. Now, how do we get bodies in his way to slow him down so the entry of the ball is delayed? We need pressure on the ball, that's critical. Too many times someone will do a great defensive job on the post, but the guy defending the ball is a lazy bones and the ball gets in easily. You need everyone working on the same page.

Phil gives the players a lot of scope for contribution. For instance, if I'm guarding a guy and Phil wants a double team from the baseline and I feel it would be better coming from the top, it's me doing the work and guarding him, so Phil will say, 'Okay we'll make that adjustment until I see you're getting beaten.'

In the Orlando series, they wanted to double team Shaq. I wanted to go one-on-one and I got my way and we were able to stay with it. 'Okay,' Phil obliged, 'we'll go one-on-one until it's hurting us, then we'll do this.' It's a give-and-take situation. Phil's won a lot, a championship as a player with the Knicks and four as a coach with us, and another in the CBA with Albany Patroons. He's been Coach of the Year, too, just last season, yet his ego's not such that he thinks he knows it all.

For each team, we have a new set of rules. In the NBA, the players and coaches are so good, you can't simply have the same basic rules to follow and just 'play and see what happens'. We adjust our game-plan every game, substantially sometimes. It gets much more cerebral as the season wears on.

During a play-off day, we can spend up to an hour and a half on the court and an hour in the video room just seeing what they do and come game time, it enables us to take opponents out of their rhythm.

You get a feel for the gym, the floor, the nets, the courts, the background. Usually we'll often play shooting games at the end of shootarounds for our fine money. We have a fine system called silly fines, and you're busted if you don't wear the right gear for practice or if you're late for the bus. There are a number of things—plane situations, what you wear on the road— that could be a silly fine. But I think Dennis has shut that whole dress code system down. Dresses were never in the rule book. A silly fine is $50. You get a silly fine for the first five minutes then it's a real life Bulls' fine, more like $250. Missed practice, it's more like ... I don't know, because I've never missed practice. Silly fines happen every day, it gets to a couple hundreds bucks in the pot.

The coaches adjudicate and pick the shoot-out teams. They split us up in to four groups, so it's always pretty evenly spread. We play a round robin spot shooting game, winners get the dough. Assistant coach Jimmy Rodgers handles the fine money and waits until he thinks the pot's big enough. It gets you shooting under pressure in the same situations in the arena. It's game tempo because you want to get up as many shots as you can—and make as many. Hey, there's money on the line, although the pot never has more than $300–400. It wouldn't get bigger than that. If it did, we'd put it into a kitty for a party or something.

I can't sleep more than an hour on game days. I have a meal around 1pm, with one of the guys. There are some pretty unconventional pregame meal routines too. Bill likes donuts and cola and Mike always eats a steak, that's almost taboo if you talk to the nutritionists. I read a bit, but don't watch much television, I prefer to go for a walk usually, something to keep my body active, walk lunch off, maybe go to a mall. You always need something like a new book, postcard or whatever, it's a reason to have a walk, and check out the city. I'll head back to the hotel and have a snooze. The bus is usually ready to roll at 4.30–5pm.

I'm usually one of the first on the bus and take a coffee with me—the team drinks a lot of it. There are always jugs of coffee in the locker room before the game and almost to a man, the guys will drink coffee. Surprising maybe to some, but caffeine is a very integral part of the NBA lifestyle. Scottie and Michael will drink a couple of cups before the game. Apparently it enhances your stamina and ability to process whatever you need, I don't know. It's a stimulant, it kickstarts the body and wakes you up.

We get to the arena 90 minutes to two hours before the game. We hang out, get dressed, get taped, go out and shootaround again for 30–45 minutes. I'll work on my post game, work on my short range jump shot, I got a lot of those last year. It became a staple diet to an extent. Michael always knows if he hits with the pass on the flare out on the baseline, I'm going to knock down 60 per cent of them. Pregame I'll make maybe 50 of those and then hit 20 free throws, and throw a few hooks.

I like to break a bit of a sweat

before heading back to the locker to put my uniform on.

My pre-game shootaround is timed to perfection and for a reason. I go out on court when the media is in the locker room. I always regard the locker room as a sanctuary to focus before the game, but the media is allowed in there up to 45 minutes before the game begins. It's a function for the media, particularly in the cities we visit, to work on

ON THE ROAD WITH THE BEATLES

The media is always there, even before a game.

feature material with Michael, Scottie and Dennis, or any of us really.

Plus, most beat writers must fill early edition papers with stories, before rewriting the game story into the same hole. So they are always sniffing around for something. Because we're so popular with the media, it's a frenzy. I have to push my bag under the chair so no-one treads on it. I'll spend 10 minutes answering questions and then go to shoot. That's the only way I can focus.

It's a media-driven industry and I appreciate that and we need it, but I'll do it after the game. Any athlete will tell you that right before he/she competes, you need to have a certain amount of room. At home obviously we can go to back rooms the media can't get access to. Moreover, we're often treating injuries so I'm in treating a knee or whatever niggle I have at the time.

The team is in 45 minutes before tip-off, and Phil will go over things we discussed that day, and anything he changed his mind on, which he does a lot. Then it's game time. After that it's the media again. On the road, we'll give them 20–25 minutes, but usually we have to fly out to the next city, so there's no mucking around.

Michael, as usual, knows the game and spends as much time as the media needs. He's a media darling. We'll normally have a few beers on the bus after the game. If we're playing the next night I normally wouldn't, but a couple of guys do. Michael will have one or two on the bus, but if it's a big game the next day, probably not.

If we have a game on the road the next day, obviously we'll fly right out. If we have a game on the road two days later, we'll stay in town, and it's back to the hotel, the limos are waiting and the boys are going out. If we're going home we fly straight out. It's uncommon to stay the night anywhere if it's not necessary. Three quarters of the time we're flying straight out. The NBA is all about what's next, not what has been. But if we stay in town, those are the sort of the nights Phil says, 'Okay boys, let your hair down.' It's a chance to go out. He likes to do that in Miami, it's a good town for that.

We have a guy in Boston that works with us on awareness techniques as well as relaxation techniques and meditation. He's worked mostly with guys in prison and helps them dealing with the anxiety and the anger of prison and how they can, first, be aware of it, and, second, control it and get back into themselves. For some reason he sees a lot of parallels between them and us. Maybe it's the gladiatorial aspect of it, who knows.

It's been good though, very beneficial. Whenever we're in Boston and occasionally when he comes to Chicago as he did during the play-offs, we meet with him instead of shootaround, but often we'll couple it with shootaround. We'll even do some yoga, experience different poses, some body relaxing, getting the body awake, and we do it for nearly an hour. Michael and Scottie, the leaders of the team, really get into it and they enjoy it. They'll be the first ones with their eyes closed. Legend has it that Phil one day busted Michael peeking to see if his teammates were concentrating. We were and he quickly got back into it. It's not a giggling affair at all where guys make fun of it. I think the boys really appreciate it. It's a bit of an oasis in the NBA.

The road is work and we worked it better than anyone else in NBA history en route to the title.

But it's always nice to get home.

chapter 10

class act

Out of everyone on the team, Scottie is the most giving,

even if he's not playing very well. He had patches this year when he struggled, but he was always conscious to focus a lot on getting other guys involved on the team. By nature he's a very giving sort of bloke and that makes him fun to be with. And it makes him a good leader because the guys respect him for that.

There's a lot of talk of how hard Michael practises and the intensity he brings to practice. MJ obviously draws a lot of attention, but Scottie's right there with him every step of the way, he's the guy that pushes Mike every single time they step on the practice floor. Come game night, Scottie's the guy that we often give the toughest defensive assignment to. He can guard anything from the point man to the streaky, three-man with hops.

Remember back to the 1991 Finals against LA, it was Pip's defence on Magic Johnson that won the Bulls the series and their first NBA title. He's a workhorse for us and if you need someone on the glass, Scottie's right there too. He pushes the ball up the floor for us with that long, loping stride. He's the ultimate do-it-all guy.

He deserves a bit more respect than he gets because Scottie has definitely accomplished a hell of a lot in the NBA and done it the hard

82

Nobody finishes on the break like Pip.

SCOTTIE PIPPEN

Scottie feels no pain.

way. He's a superstar now, but is a player who didn't get spoonfed with a fully paid scholarship at college. He was a team manager for the first year before breaking his way into a team and proving himself at NCAA level. So of all the all-star types, Pip appreciates where he's at in more ways than most because he's seen it from the outside.

He's become a very good friend to me and is certainly a lot closer to me than Michael. Out of all of them I talk to Scottie the most. I'm mates with Dennis, but it's more like have a couple of beers, slap you on the back, bump chests, head-butt ra-ra-ra. But I'll talk to Scottie about what's going on in the team and other things. He and Kelly have struck up a good friendship and he's been over to our place a fair bit working on his computer, getting it all hooked up on the Internet.

His public image is very different to his real image, he's mild mannered, a soft sort of unimposing bloke.

The first year without MJ on the team was very difficult for Scottie, you saw that through the play-off frustration when he sat out the last 1.8 seconds of a game against New York in 1994 when Phil ran a play for Toni and not Pip. There was a lot to deal with in coping with the expectations of leading a successful club and being thrust into the spotlight in Michael's absence. He obviously didn't handle it as well as he would have liked.

Before MJ's retirement, Scottie had to play in Michael's shadow and rightly so, but had he been on any other team, he would have been the focus. He had to work hard to get his recognition and yet he was like a younger brother in a sense that he never had to get out front and take charge.

But last year he did a great job of being the team leader. I found him to be completely professional in what he did. He's the most professional among us in many ways. This year I think it was actually an ideal situation where Michael was saying it was Scottie's team. Scottie still had a better rapport with a lot of the guys because we'd known him longer and yet Michael was there to back him up or to take control in certain situations. ○

RUNNING WITH THE BULLS

Enforcing a point with D Rod.

LUC LONGLEY

Rare air for me.

RUNNING WITH THE BULLS

The right hook was a handy weapon.

LUC LONGLEY

Playing above the rim in the finals.

chapter 11

the marathon begins

When the season started we knew we were going to be good, we knew we had all the pieces and we had the leaders. It was six months to a potential NBA championship, yet it felt tantalisingly close already. The promise of what lay ahead kept us all excited and even more focused.

Phil and the coaching staff made some critical moves in the summer preceding the 1995–96 season which reshaped the way we would play. Management knew it had to get Ron Harper back in the flow. Ronnie had just come off a wasted season where he found himself languishing on the bench after the return of Jordan and was a non-factor in our offence. And this was a guy who poured in 20 points a night regularly for Cleveland and then the Clippers. He was a big guard with long arms who could definitely work the defence. He had loads of talent and Phil instructed him to work hard over the summer because he was going to start him.

Rebounding was still a worry for us though, after losing Horace Grant to free agency. Toni had been starting at power forward, but was out of position and boarding was not his forte. Phil recognised Toni would be of most benefit coming off the bench, giving us some instant impact where he creates match-up problems with his height and deadly perimeter game. Toni didn't like the idea, his ego was telling him he should be starting. But Phil convinced him there was a crucial role for him off the bench in the mould of former Celtics great Kevin McHale, who didn't start, but was a perennial all-star and helped his team win

LUC LONGLEY

Hi-Ho, Hi-Ho...

championships.

There were questions how it would all pan out, but I think Dennis answered most of those once he signed and started to play. While we knew we were good, we weren't quite sure just how good, we just went in and started hoopin'. Everyone expected us to dominate. Bill Walton came in to training camp doing some work for broadcaster NBC and said he expected us to be

one of the great teams of all time.

A couple of days later Bulls beat writer Lacy Banks wrote in the *Chicago Sun Times*, predicting we would win 70 games. I remember Steve looking over at Jud and him asking 'Could we really be that good?' Jud shrugged his shoulders as if to say 'Who knows?'

We actually lost a couple of exhibition games and although they don't mean much, we certainly didn't look invincible. Then it seemed as the season progressed, we got better and better. We built on things very quickly. The remarkable thing about this team is we got tuned into each other. In past Bulls teams it would take us to the play-offs to be doing some of the more complicated offensive sets. But we were comfortable with each other very early and it started to show.

We were able to handle whatever was thrown at us and I think that

THE MARATHON BEGINS

was a function of being a very veteran-like team. A lot of guys had played together admittedly, but everything seemed to gel right away. And Dennis has a brilliant basketball mind and picked it all up very quickly. He understands the game incredibly well.

Late in the exhibition season, we were doing auditions for our battle cry 'What time is it?' and then the rest of the squad chants 'Game Time—whoo!' It's our pre-game huddle bonding session that signals the start to our night's work. Well, a couple of the guys didn't have enough bass or voice projection. We needed a new guy because it had been Cliff Levingston, then Scott Williams and Pete Myers, and now they were all playing elsewhere.

A couple of guys gave it a go. But like an impatient stage play director, 'Next' was the call. There was no heart. Then my number was called and with the oomph of Pavarotti, I bellowed 'What time is it?' and they loved it. I was on, I was the man, it was me, my job for the rest of the year and I was psyched. Until Scottie talked me in to giving them the Australian remix. I came back to them with 'What bloody time is it?' I went with it prior to warm-ups, but that was it. I got the axe right there on the spot. Randy Brown got the job the next audition and kept it all year. So Scottie owes me for that one.

We opened in November at home to Charlotte and cruised 105–91. Michael quickly answered any debate about his form with 42 points, while Dennis set the season precedent by leading our team in boards, this time though, with merely 11. We were 12-2 in the opening month, Dennis was later injured and I stepped it up on the boards late, leading the team in rebounds four times. We did lose two games on the road, to Orlando and Seattle, but there was hardly any concern.

Home.

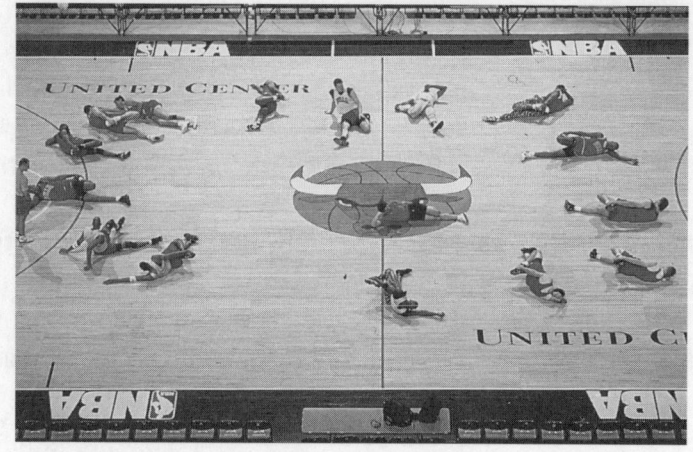

Me and my circle of friends.

In what was another marketing/merchandising brainstorm by management, they decided we'd don a different uniform as an alternative road strip—black with a red pin stripe. Whether you liked it or not, it sold like hot cakes. But on 14 November we wore them for the first time and lost at Orlando. We dropped four of the eight games in which we wore them and immediately put them back in mothballs.

After that Seattle loss 97–92, Phil was cool and as calm as ever and unperturbed. He circled the locker room as we took off our tape and prepared for the showers and media crush. He told us to taste it, savour it, stick it in our craw. I think Phil envisaged us playing Seattle in the Finals, I think he knew what was going on. Maybe it was that Swift Eagle coming through, he could see that far ahead.

I had my career high 21 points that night in Seattle. Ironically I've always played well against and in Seattle, and one of the places I've never played well is New Jersey. I don't know whether it's a climatic thing or it's just the depressive environment, whereas Seattle is more upbeat, my sort of place. I don't know. I went through patches where I was scoring in the high teens a lot and then a couple of games where it wasn't happening for me and that would peg my scoring average back. But generally, I was very involved in the offence.

December–January went almost unblemished, just a solitary slip-up to Indiana 103–97 on Boxing Day. We would atone for that with interest. Dennis returned from injury and immediately swooped on 20 rebounds against the Knicks. It was the first of three straight 20-plus rebound nights. With green hair, he led us in boards in 12 of the month's 13 games. We went through January undefeated 14–zip and it didn't look like we were going to be beaten. No-one was leaving the welcome mat out for us, but we went in to each game expecting to walk out with the W.

The closest anyone got was the Raptors, whom we beat by three, but we walloped Seattle by 29 at home, beat Houston twice and smoked the Knicks by 20. I used to quite enjoy looking at our opponents in a perverse sort of way and seeing defeat in their faces before the game even started, especially at the United Center. You could sense we were the biggest scalp they could ever possibly want, one that would be made even more meritorious on our home pine. But deep down you saw them cringing.

It was great. I had never been on a team that had that affect on players. There were some games where we weren't really as ready to play yet people gave us the game before we even won it. We didn't deserve to win a lot of the games. We bluffed our way through in a sense.

On 23 January we spanked our old enemies New York at their place 99–79 and I outplayed their all-star centre Patrick Ewing. I had 14

THE MARATHON BEGINS

Patrick gets caught looking.

points and 10 rebounds to Patrick's 10 and nine. We were 35–3 and the 70-win question raised its head yet again. Said Scottie: '70? Hell, I think we can do 75!' No-one doubted him.

Before we knew it it was all-star break. We were 42–5 and on record pace, it just crept up on us that fast. MJ and Pip were Eastern Conference starters, but there was no Dennis. Coaches felt he needed a more well-rounded game to warrant selection. Dennis alerted them to the fact when he logged his first career triple double at Philadelphia on 13 January with 10 points, 21 rebounds and 10 assists. The four days off at all-star weekend was spent at the blackjack tables in Vegas. And I guess after playing in San Antonio for a while, Dennis really wasn't too fussed about going back.

It was only February, yet the buzzword was 'Bulls', quickly followed

89

by '70 wins'. Everyone was saying we were the best team ever. It became a runaway freight train for us, but we couldn't engage the brakes, we couldn't help winning basketball games. We stumbled very rarely and when we did it angered us, we had so much pride as a group, so that the next team coming in, no matter who, was usually in big trouble. The only time we lost two games in a row was out west to Denver and then Phoenix and they didn't have me.

Missing the Olympics was one thing, but it's tough sitting out regular season games as well. Absent for the majority of a key February road trip out west, I was allowed plenty of time for reflection. We were seriously rolling and we began the trip with a win at Houston 98–87. We thought we played poorly, but blew them out anyway. They came back at the end but we had them by 20 most of the game. Mentally it was a big victory over the defending champions.

That was the game I did my knee. It was freakish really, on something you do thousands of times during the course of the year. I was just going up, caught a rebound drifting to my left a little bit, landed to go back up to my right, and when I fired to jump, my knee went click and twisted. You shouldn't get injured doing that. I bobbled the lay-up and missed it. I actually played the rest of the game. Sometimes with enough adrenalin, those sort of things don't worry you. That injury was just a function of the ankle being sore.

We flew on to Sacramento, I had tests there which came up Bad News Bears and then flew straight back to Chicago. On 1 February the boys beat the Kings 105–85 and I went on the injured list for the second time in the season. They followed that with a win over the Lakers, with Magic back in the famous No.32. I wasn't there but according to Steve, Magic didn't look that good, but they got out to a lead through adrenalin.

The crowd was over the top and scalpers were getting $1000 a ticket, it was nuts, one of the biggest nights for LA basketball. Basically, we pulled away in the second quarter and crushed them 99–84. That was one message the guys left for the league, in that 'None of this stops us'. Scottie upstaged everybody with 30 points and Dennis had one of those regulation nights with 23 boards.

Michael could sense that trip as the pivotal point of the season.

He said, 'When we went on that 18-game winning streak the team started to gel together and became confident in each other. Roles and responsibilities started to become fulfilled. From that point on, it became "How far can we take this? This is fun, let's see if we can take this further and further". Everything started to fall in to line.'

Then bang, the boys lost two straight, to the Nuggets and Suns. It was an interesting time for me to sit back and watch the team. When you're in amongst it you don't get the same perspective as you do when you sit back and get a fan's view and listen to the commentary and how people respond during the game.

The guys were at Denver and came back from 31 points down to take the lead in the fourth quarter but finally lost 105–99. Michael had 22 of his 39 in the third after we came back from 25 down at half-time and we took a 92–91 lead in the final term. An 8–0 Nuggets run killed us in the end. It snapped our 18-game winning streak, but we were still 41–4. I marvelled at the team and their effort and ability. It gave me a real sense of pride being involved with those guys.

Two nights later, we were at the Suns and Charles Barkley was fired up. He threw an elbow at Dennis, they were lined up next to each other, and copped Dennis right in the ribs. The ref gave Charles a tech and after the T, Charles looked at the ref and said 'f... you, f... you, f... you', according to Steve. The ref said nothing and Charles went off again 'f... you, f... you, f... you' and the ref wouldn't do anything. And apparently KJ, Kevin Johnson, turned to Steve and said 'Can you believe that, anyone else in the league would be thrown out.' That's Charles Barkley doing his thing. They won it 106–96. He had 35 points and 16 boards and was talking it up that yes, we could certainly be beaten in the run to the championship.

Phil seemed unfazed about the two glitches on our season record.

Where the hard work is done.

LUC LONGLEY

That's high for me.

'We're not as worried about this as you might think,' he said. Why should we have been? We had just won 18 straight games before those two losses. All was well within our camp, no worries.

The fact they lost the only two games in a row in the regular season immediately I left the team, highlighted not only in the public's mind, but with guys like Michael, my worth to the club. A lot of the work I do is not necessarily on a highlight reel or a statistic, but both Michael and Scottie came up to me after that trip and said

'When are you coming back? We need ya man.

Get it right because we want you for the rest of the season.' That made me feel good and I think that was probably the first time during the course of the season when either of those guys recognised how much I was doing on their behalf.

I worked my arse off during the two and half week period, keeping in shape in the swimming pool, doing everything extra that I could so when I returned I was right to go. To still be in good shape after that sort of injury is difficult, but I came right back in, started, playing 25 minutes a game. We blew away Cleveland at home 102-76. I had stayed in really good shape, mostly through work in the pool.

When the team was out west and again when I was injured in late March, the only thing I could do for cardio-vascular work was swimming in the therapy pool with a rope tied around my waist and a vest strapped to my chest. Boring, but necessary. About four feet in front of me at the far end, there's a pool depth sign right on the water line that reads 8' 0 IN, for eight feet, no inches. But looking

Home sweet home.

at the '0 IN' for inches, with the water level dissecting the lettering half way up, in my mind I was imagining it was the O apostrophe N of O'Neal and I was wearing him down.

Shaq and the Magic is where we faltered last year and I knew that was what Michael and Scottie were focusing on in terms of getting to the Finals, first through Orlando. So I used that as a focus, someone to chase, just playing through scenarios on the court. The work I was

LUC LONGLEY

Good to practise at home after a tough week in Seattle.

doing in the pool, battling to reach an impossible target physically, but mentally a very attainable one, was enabling me to get by him, stop him, block his shot, whatever. I was spending 45 minutes a day in there alone, churning away in the pool. I would lift too, but I was getting really bored with the guys away on the road. It gave me a train of thought. And I think it planted a real seed of looking toward the play-offs at that point of the year.

There's nothing like playing, but watching is kind of fun. I don't get to watch my team very much, I'm always out there doing it, it really was a different experience. That was one of the first times I realised how good we were. Looking at it from a distance, Wow! They have all the pieces, but hey, they needed a big centre in there. Bill was doing a good job offensively, but defensively it's a different story and that was my role, to anchor the defence.

As early as March, when we were 54–6, Steve Kerr made a spot-on assessment of our club and its title chances. We knew back then a championship was ours. We conceded teams could sneak up and get us in one game during the play-offs, but nobody in the NBA could beat us four times in a series. Our confidence was knocking down doors and we were still three months away from the Finals.

And Phil said it best when asked by a TV crew if he thought we'd win. He said we had all the pieces and that we'd done everything right, we'd worked harder than any group he'd been around. There was no reason why we wouldn't win. And there wasn't.

THE MARATHON BEGINS

It was probably three quarters of the way through the season when me, Jud and Steve were sitting on the plane having a couple of beers, thinking we were bad arses. We'd just crushed someone and with the next couple of days off, we decided we'd get tattoos—after the season—to remember the remarkable year that was unfolding. It was going to be one of those bonding things between the three of us who are pretty tight. We all share a bank of three lockers at home games,

we're the three Amigos.

The design was part of the issue, we wanted something that said 72-10 or 'champs' on an ankle or something. Jud wanted something really minuscule on his butt where no-one could see it. We had to run it by the girls and sure enough, no go, all bets are off. Jud's in-laws and wife went ballistic and said 'There's no way you're getting a tattoo.' He whimped out on the deal. Steve and I couldn't go ahead with it just the two of us, the pact had been made for three, but Jud just disintegrated on us, he folded.

The season was full of lighter moments, it was like one big school holiday, just a great time. We were relaxed, we were winning and having fun. I've never been on a team—even an Australian national team—that had quite the same social fabric within the team. We were just very close. I don't think that's normal in the NBA—at least not in my experience.

We just couldn't wait for the next game, the boys were grinnin' and loving it. Phil would have to call practice off. 'Sorry guys, I don't want to burn you out for tomorrow night.' We were right into it, the juggernaut was rolling and nothing you put in front of it was going to stop it. It had developed its own momentum and it was full steam ahead. We couldn't get guys off the court, on to the bus and back to the hotel when we were on the road. No-one wanted to go back to the hotel and slum around to kill time. We wanted to stay there and play basketball, stay there until the tip-off.

There's a little MJ in there somewhere.

There were some speed bumps though, some reality checks that rattled us like shock treatment, games which re-ignited the absolute optimum focus, which can wane slightly when you're simply crushing teams. We felt through the course of the year people thought it was simple to win, that it was easy for us.

March brought us a 12-2 record, and we got through Dennis's six-game head-butt suspension with a 5-1 record as Michael led us in rebounding five times. But two losses stuck with us. The Knicks spanked us by 32 points at the Garden, our worst loss for the year by a mile. Two weeks later the fans were in shock but for a different reason. We lost to an expansion team, Toronto 109-108.

It showed we could lose to anybody

and it showed us then, that every night is work for us. That's what made it amazing, we were up for every game and we won 72 times during the regular season and to know a Toronto could beat us made us sit up again. The look in the guys' eyes was 'Never again', but in many ways it was good for us, it taught us we weren't invincible.

It was those sorts of experiences when I could sense the players' resolve kick in and the two games following the Raptors' debacle were an 111-80 win over Atlanta and then we roughed up the Clips 106-85. March was finally over and we were into the home stretch.

In early April, the last month of the regular season grind, we could see that resolve and focus in Phil starting to kick in too. The month opened with two straight games with Miami, away and home, and that's why—Heat coach Pat Riley. Phil respects him, but it's obvious to us who have played for him that there's a special dislike, a fierce, perhaps bitter rivalry there and Phil is always super focused when they clash. When we play against Riley he cares more about those games.

We had two game-free days before the first clash at Miami Arena. Where we would sometimes in similar situations get one of those days off as a recuperation day, we now practised for two and a half hours each day. There was a bit of play-off atmosphere because we were watching videos and had a scout team (second five) playing the Miami offence. It was full-on. Again, like in Seattle when we dropped our regular season game to the Sonics at their gym, I think Phil believed we would end up playing Miami in the play-offs, but it was even more than that.

We'd been beaten once down there in late February. The Heat dressed only eight players after making two trades and Rex Chapman got off with 9-of-10 threes for 39 points and they ate us up 113-104. That really riled Phil, pardon the pun. That night MJ and Scottie were a

THE MARATHON BEGINS

combined 13-39 from the floor. So before the Miami game down there in April, Phil challenged us and declared, 'I don't think you can win in Miami. You're not good enough.'

I remember the guys looking around the locker room with frowns on our faces saying 'Bullshit!' That was an insult. We were 62-8 at that stage and thought 'What are you talking about?' But it had the desired effect. It got the boys fired up and we crushed them 110-92 and again two days later at home, 100-92.

The Journey is the Reward, remember.

We finally slipped up at home to Charlotte on 8 April, 98-87. We'd beaten the Hornets by 30 after taking a 20-0 start just three days earlier and we slept on them a bit and they got us. What made it more surprising was we murdered them on the boards 51-31 and couldn't convert all that possession. Phil, again being the master of turning a seemingly negative, bummer situation in to a positive, explained to the press, 'I told the guys I wasn't disappointed. It let them know going into the play-offs that we are not impervious on our home court. It's good to have reality set in.' Still, the 44-game win streak at home was over and so was the goal of becoming the first team to sweep at home 41-0 in a single season.

Reality did set in again a week later. The 70-win game was in Milwaukee, which is only a 45 minute bus ride, in fact it's the only bus ride we take all year. We were on our way up there and people were virtually hanging off the freeway overpasses with signs, people were driving beside us with signs, it looked more like a presidential parade. There was a massive procession following us up there, even two or three TV news helicopters hovering above us getting the OJ-like footage of the bus travelling up the freeway.

A brief moment to catch up.

We got to the game and all that attention and hype had sucked the energy out of us. We came out flatter than a CD and it took us over three quarters to get the blood flowing. We were terrible in the third quarter and I was carrying us, I was the only Bull who had anything going offensively and Phil gave me a lot of credit for keeping us in that game. But down the stretch, when we are so clinical, we were just too good, although they gave us a run for our money. That almost made it more fun because it was more a battle and we felt like we had to win it the hard way to really deserve it.

We finally got there 86–80 and so became the first team to win 70 games in an NBA season.

In the locker room afterwards it was all cigars, cigars are a big thing with the boys these days, in fact Johnny Salley has opened up a cigar shop in Chicago. Michael likes to smoke a cigar, he makes no pretences about that, as long as it's a very good Cuban cigar.

I didn't ride the bus back. Jud's wife had brought up his monstrous eight-seater suburban 4WD, it's as big as an earth mover. So on the return leg, Jud, Steve, Toni and I and our wives piled in with beers and cigars for the roadie home. We stopped at a little hole in the wall near where Steve lives called the Lantern Tavern for a few frosties to toast our well-deserved record.

Pip enjoys a victory stogie.

The locals were hanging out, knocking back a few quiet ones when we showed up and transformed the place in to a hoppin' party. The fans were hyped and then Phil strolled in later, chuffing on a cigar. He was as proud as a peacock. It had been a triumphant night and we kicked on well into the am hours and Detroit was in town 36 hours later.

That was probably the first time we let our hair down in a sense in achieving one of the milestones. We didn't like to admit to ourselves that the regular season win record was one of our focuses. We said '70 wins. We don't care.' Dennis labelled it a 'stupid goal'. But we did care, you could tell by the reaction of the players. It was like we'd won Lotto, it was huge for us.

Michael said: 'People have no idea what sort of pressure we've been under, having everyone in the league gearing the whole season around beating you, night after night.

This puts our names in the history books,

but it doesn't have the same effect as winning a championship.' Mike would know. I didn't have a clue what it was like.

Once we reached the much talked about and anticipated 70-win

THE MARATHON BEGINS

plateau, we deflated a little bit, although we did smoke the Pistons 110–79. But a couple of guys took time off for injury maintenance and we lost only our second home game of the year, this time to Indiana by a point. We'd achieved so many goals, we were starting to reload for the Finals and really didn't come out and take care of business, particularly with Reggie Miller missing, out with a fractured orbital of the right eye.

Indiana is a legitimate team, they were the only team besides Seattle to beat us twice and took home some major scalps before falling short in the play-offs. But we were pegging it back a notch, Phil was playing the bench an awful lot, resting Michael and myself. By this stage it was a real nursing act with my knees. I'd had a cortisone shot at that stage to carry me through the play-offs.

There was nothing to gain by winning in the final week, except for various records. Now we were attempting to match Boston's home court record of 40–1, while we already had the win percentage record in the bag. Those sort of things were not as important as preparing for the play-offs. We dropped a squeaker to the Pacers 100–99 and now there was one game to go, on the road to Washington.

At the beginning of the season Toni was talking shit about how he was a better free throw shooter than I was, despite the fact I whopped his arse a year earlier when I went .822 to his feeble .748. His argument and challenge had about as much substance as his shot selection at times, but it was worth further debate. So I said 'Righto, let's make a bet on it.' We came to the conclusion that a case of Dom Perignon champagne was an appropriate bet so we could drink it during the celebrations.

We both took slim leads through the course of the season and took the pleasure of telling the other all about it. Toni of course, seeing more of the ball, got to the line more as well, but this was a bet on percentage only, not free throws made and attempted. In typical Hollywood fashion, it came down to the very last game of the regular season and we were tied at .772.

As is the norm, the Bulls like to look for me early in games and I got to line and nailed two of two and I could immediately sense the urgency in Toni's game, he was desperate, he just had to beat me. The champers meant nothing, nor did the cover price, Toni's on a $26 million contract. This was a pride thing.

Toni stepped up the intensity. He's driving hard going to the hole, leaning in to people, he's chucking up garbage and he can't get a call. He never gets to the line and I win the bet. My two gimmes nudged my percentage up by .005 to .777. A case of champagne arrived at my locker two days later. We would drink most of it during the post play-off celebrations. I shared it around a bit, Steve and his wife Margot spent some time at our place and yes, Toni and his wife got to sample some of the winnings also.

If that wasn't enough, Australia's win over Croatia at the Olympics gave me a whole season's worth of ammunition for trash talkin'. It is going to be fun.

It was good to have the grind of the regular season out of the way. Now the fun part of the season, the gravy, was on us. In the locker room and around each other, we say 'It's a marathon not a sprint'. Pace yourself early and be ready for the dash at the end. That's Bulls' time.

Once the regular season is over, you've earned your salary, you've taken care of the TV requirements, all the hard bits. The end of the season is the players' reward. It was great to have the play-offs on the doorstep with home court advantage, all bodies intact, pride intact and feeling good about ourselves.

The shirts the team adopted to maintain focus in the Finals.

The Bulls signed me to accomplish two things: take up some space in the middle and to combat the opposition monoliths in the play-offs, when it comes time to really bang bodies and put it on the line, just as veteran Bill Cartwright had done before me. The coaching staff has often said, 'Luc, we want you to paint yourself after Bill Cartwright'. They've brought 'Teach' back as an assistant coach, he was great for me to play with for half a year, studying his moves, his tricks and all the things he did well.

There was a play-off blueprint the Bulls had schemed and it appeared it would pan out as expected. Great for management and coaches, but crappy for me. If everything worked out like it should, I was getting a trio of stiffs named Alonzo Mourning, Patrick Ewing and then Shaq. After that I didn't care, if we got that far I was going on holiday, or so I thought.

It was when we were right on the precipice of the play-offs, that Scottie and Ron coined the phrase

72-10 '...DON'T MEAN A THING WITHOUT THE RING'.

They copyrighted it and it became the hottest selling t-shirt in town. All the guys on the team got one to wear. It was our way of putting our accomplishments to the side and starting afresh. ○

chapter 12
breaking the tedium

The season gets very long, very tedious, you're around the same guys all season. Because there are no weekends for an NBA player, it becomes very monotonous in a sense. Practical joking this year actually boiled over and became ridiculous, but it became one of the ways to help us punctuate the time. In fact kidding around became rather important.

I showed up to practice one day and something didn't seem quite right, like when your house has been burgled for the first time—you know something's out of place, but for a couple of seconds you're not quite sure. Every door and every common room spot had a photocopied picture of a naked bodybuilder with this really little penis and my head delicately superimposed on top. And the caption read 'Put my little shrimp on your barbie'. That was the boys having a bit of a go at me. There would have been 30 photos in the practice facility. It wasn't hard to know who was the culprit—Steve and Jud, my boys.

Sledding with that pair became an enjoyable pastime. It was also an integral part of

A night on the slopes with Jud and Steve wasn't so kind to the sled.

the entertainment program for my international guests. In Chicago there's a mountainous slope that is brilliant for sledding under lights. After one game, me, Jud and Steve hit this slope with a couple of Australian mates, Chris Appleby and Tim Morrissey (a 1990 Boomers teammate), a couple of former NBL hoopers. It would have been 20 degrees below but we had some rum and port to warm the cockles. On the last run, we had a serious spill, one sled crashing in to the other. Both sleds were casualties, the bodies stayed intact.

All the Bulls craziness started with some small things to loosen up practice. This game has developed where Steve and Jud and any other guard will try to get out on the court after weights before any of the big guys and make a lay-up, any shot on the main practice court. Big guys will try to do the same thing. It's a sort of subterfuge thing. So the big guys will try to knock the ball out of mid air, get their own ball and make a lay-up. It's just a stupid thing. We're all in the weights room together first and will be heading that way, and guys will hide behind the curtains and wait for others, it just lightens up practice.

Well it became big guys vs small guys. Me and Bill against Steve and Jud basically. Jack Haley would get involved but we were never quite sure which side he was on, he would just throw his ball anywhere as long as there was a ball going up. That's where the big guys–small guys thing started.

In February the season's getting long, so Steve and Jud got the ball rolling and decided to freeze Bill's underwear during practice. They wet it, laid it out and put it in the freezer. Well, I got wind of it through the strength coach and turned it around on them being on Bill's side. I got his boxers, put them under hot water, melted the ice, then put them in the dryer and hung them in Bill's locker.

Jud and Steve came laughing back to the locker after practice thinking they are going to see a huge joke and there's Bill putting on his nice, dry, warm underwear. I was injured, so I had nothing to do during practice except lift weights and swim in the pool. I did the switch while everyone else was on the practice floor.

Getting one up on Steve and Jud is a major accomplishment and it's important to make it a good one, because you know they're coming back at ya with something special. I decided to take it one step further during a home game. I grabbed Steve's and Jud's underwear, wet them and put them on a tray, on coat-hangers, which, if you can believe it, is what they do with their underwear. I froze them, then hung them back up. We all came back in to the locker room after the game and they are trying to get dressed in a hurry before the media busts its way in. They reach in for their underwear and see it frozen solid.

I had the equipment manager, Johnny Ligmanowsk, do the deed.

BREAKING THE TEDIUM

Jud discovers the chilling truth.

Their undies were frozen, like a plank. The media was on their way in right then so they had to free-ball it. I was out of there very quickly.

Johnny, or Sweets as we call him because he's a got a jolly figure and always got gum in his pockets, has become very involved in the practical jokes, in fact he's become the master. He got Jack Haley a cheerleader of the year award trophy and presented it to him at the last game of the season. It had a cheergirl with a pom pom on top because Jack really didn't play much but did a lot of cheering.

Jack was the butt of a lot of practical jokes, including the first game that Jack played. Management took pity on him and decided they'd better play him once before the season ended. There were two games left and they had to pull out his uniform and Michael's asking him 'So what number are you Jack?' No-one had a clue, because he'd never put a uniform on.

One thing about Michael is he is hard on his teammates.

Jack doesn't play much.

He's not one to mince words and I think he had a certain amount of frustration with Jack at times for the role he played, a cheerleader and nothing else. I remember Jack was getting on the bus and Michael yelling from the back, over the whole din of the bus 'Jack, what are you doing here, do you have tickets for the game?' Another time Jack stopped outside the bus to give autographs to kids and Michael popped his head over the chair in front and chirped, 'Jack, they only want autographs from players!' It's safe to say, Michael had no time for Jack, nor did Scottie. Neither did I.

I guess Jack simply gave us plenty of ammunition. When Jack was ready to suit up for his season finale in the locker room, Johnny had strung fake spider webs all over Jack's locker. Just another dig at his lack of input this year and the fact his locker lay dormant for 10 months. Jack ranked low on the respect quotient. Then when Jack was on the bench and getting ready to get in the game, Michael and Scottie had stashed a couple of photographic equipment air dusters under their chairs. They both stood up and started spraying Jack and his uniform off, because he'd been in hibernation all year. Alas, it must have been a tight game, he never played. Jack did play one solitary game,

BREAKING THE TEDIUM

scoring five points and grabbing two rebounds. Jerry Krause finally released him, his baby sitting days are over.

Incensed by my magnificent underwear performance, Steve and Jud had retaliation on their minds. At that stage I had a big luxurious black 500SEL Mercedes with tinted windows, great for cruising to the game. And I noticed a big WHAM sticker plastered across the back bumper bar. It was there about a week and I hadn't noticed. I knew it was Jud and Steve. I used to pick Jud up to go to home games, so I went in to Kelly's CD collection and sure enough, there it was: 'Wake me up before you go-go', a Wham superhit of the early 80s. I rock up to Jud's and the music was pumping, and it was like 'What sticker? I love Wham.'

I gave credit to Jud for originality. Now it was on, battle lines were drawn, full metal jacket. I was injured with knee problems, what else? and the boys were back on the road, a nice time for further retaliation. I quietly put an open can of tuna in the very bottom of Jud's locker and let it fester away. It was a six-day road trip but it took him two weeks to find it I think, it got really ripe. But we weren't finished with Jud yet.

It felt like we hadn't hit warm weather in months. Our big Western Conference road swing was in November. It was now April and after walloping Charlotte 126–92, in fact leading that game 20–0, we had a couple of beers on the plane to Orlando and wanted to go out once we touched down. The Orlando accommodation is great, maybe the best on the road, it's called Grand Cypress Villas. It's a golf course resort, all rooms are independent, with little gardens surrounding them, quite private and comfortable. It was the last Orlando game of the regular season.

We wanted to get Jud to come out with us. He'd arrived at his room before his bag had been delivered by the bellman. We were outside pounding on his door and his bag was still sitting outside on the mat and he was bunkered inside. So we started rifling through his gear and started hanging all his stuff, jocks, socks, shoes in this tree outside his villa room.

Unwinding on the plane.

When we get to those warm cities we get high spirited. Because we play so much on the east coast, New Jersey, Washington, Chicago, Minnesota, Philly, New York, Boston, Detroit, Cleveland, just horrible cities during the winter, we get to Orlando and Miami and the boys spark up, they're ready to go. Where's Jud? He's hiding in his room, so we punished him.

The next night, we had a couple more beers and found a golf ball and played hand golf, basically throwing the golf ball around the course for something to do because we're stir crazy at night time. It was me, Bill and Steve. And the residual grudge from the big vs small became evident again. We ended chasing Steve all over the golf course, finally grabbing him and holding him over a sprinkler. These were the high energy, industrial strength sprinklers that shoot out 40 feet and we doused him. Bill and I each had hold of an arm and a leg, we stepped over the jet spray and then lowered him into it. He's never forgiven me for that.

That's how involved it got, the pranks got totally ridiculous. Jack was hiding people's shoes for no reason but it soon died. The play-offs were coming up, but even though we were letting our hair down and mucking around, we didn't lose focus. Against the Magic on 7 April, Shaq arrived after tip-off and tending to some personal business, but his appearance meant little and we beat them 90–86.

Another message had been sent to the NBA.

chapter 13

posting up in the post season

Eastern Conference elimination
vs Miami, 3–0

Miami was a good challenge for us because Pat Riley was in charge which translates to a very aggressive, rough style of defence and play. We were going to see that at New York anyway if everything went to plan. The Heat chalkboard prior to Game One read: NO LAYUPS. PRESSURE AND BODY THEM. It was shaping as a bruising series, and having played against Riley-coached teams before at NY, that didn't surprise me.

Miami had less depth of talent, but they had beaten us in the regular season and so they had earned our respect. It was really a testing time for me. The crux of big centre basketball in the NBA is this: if he can dominate his man offensively, it forces the double team and in a bastardised NBA offence, once you've been forced to double team, you're playing three-on-four on the back side and then you're automatically compromised.

So the challenge for me was not to let the big guys get off, guard them one-on-one once they got the ball down low and hold them, so we wouldn't have to compromise our defence. It would be the secret of our success.

My first challenge was Alonzo Mourning who has the ability to face up from 18 feet and shoot jump shots and also power in on the post.

LUC LONGLEY

Recognise any of these men?

In the first two games I/we held him to 10 and then 14 points, which basically eliminated their offence. It was a cakewalk for us through defensive emphasis, stopping him go through the lane on his left shoulder and closing out hard on his jump shots.

I didn't score a lot but that was beside the point really. In the third game, they were obviously resigned to the fact they weren't going to win the series, they had their stud centre they were going to get shots for no matter what and they brought the ball to him every time down the floor. He hit a couple of jump shots early and ended up scoring 30 but we won 112–91.

They sacrificed everything in order to make Alonzo look good.

He was getting ready to make $100m and people were starting to say 'Hey, is he worth it? He's small, and he's not getting the job done against Luc Longley.' That third game was a shame, but it wasn't bad.

Scottie was talking shit and was grandstanding the point that he was only going to take one suit to Miami in the belief we'd only be there one night to wrap up the series. Scottie can't help himself, he loves to get little media feuds going, to get people revved up, and it was an easy thing to do from the position of strength that we had, where we were the hot favourites. It was easy to talk shit, and I was a bit disappointed in him for that, but that's Scottie. But good trashers back it up—he had 22 points, 18 rebounds and 10 assists as he helped send the Heat off the court and on to the fairways.

It was really nice to beat a Pat Riley team in the Finals, too and I know Phil would have felt the same way. I don't know if Riley's a nice guy or not, because I don't really know him. But I have suffered defeats at the hands of Pat before and his style of basketball during the 1993–94 post-season when he was with New York. It was really nice to see them go down. It was a solid first step towards the championship and I think it prepared us for what was to come, which was a much wiser and experienced team in the Knicks.

Eastern Conference semis
vs New York, 4–1

Patrick Ewing has always been one of those players I've had immense respect for but usually done a fairly good job against—relatively speaking. We had one game this year where I shut him down and outscored him, which was a career highlight for me. But it's a satisfying night when I keep him below his averages, and that's pretty much what happened through the New York series.

Although in the game they beat us in OT and one other game, he hit some miraculous shots down the stretch after having been kept quiet all game. Like fade-away 25-footers with one hand up each nostril and he hit nothing but net. Or a couple of runners across the lane where I was on the ball, he pulled it back sideways, took the shot, landed on the ground, and made the hoop. It was incredible. He did a similar thing on Scottie later, when I had fouled out in the loss.

I was quite vocal in that series, both to the press and the referees regarding Patrick's constant, yet rarely called travelling violations. I got to a point in the New York series when I was guarding him and instead of having my hands up in his face, I had both hands pointing at his feet, pleading with the referees. He's the beneficiary of some generous travelling calls, the NBA's famous for it.

A fan's eye view of a play-off jam.

He gets away with it like no other which makes it hard to guard him, because playing defence is a lot about knowing which one's his pivot foot and what he can do with it and shutting down a potential move by thinking of it before he does. You look really bad if you're playing his pivot foot one way and all of a sudden he changes it and goes the other way.

I tried not to complain about that, but I did make an issue about it in the play-offs. In fact in one of the games down the stretch, we got the call, a big possession. The Knicks look to Patrick to keep them in the game or put them ahead, I can't quite remember exactly, but they gave me the call. Obviously it got through.

Of all the centres, Patrick has the best ability to make contact with his elbow, with his shoulder, with his chest even and still make the shot.

He'll plough straight in to you, bouncing off you, fading away and hitting the shot and a lot of the time drawing the foul. He's a very hard guy to keep out of foul trouble, they go to him a lot and use him as such a focal point of the offence, just like Alonzo and Shaq, but somehow more so, and he does a great job of taking a run at you.

He'll aim for the outside of your shoulder, clip you and make it look as though you forced the contact. He's very clever at it and I guess that's part of being a veteran. He's one of the best centres in the NBA, and he's a fierce competitor, he takes no backwards steps, real intense. I like Patrick, I think over the last couple of years I've gained a lot of respect from him.

Before the all-star break when I was having a good game against him at the Garden, Scottie was talking a lot of shit to Patrick at the end of the night, like 'You can't score on Luc'. At this stage Patrick's got like five points (he went 5-17) and Scottie got up him, he's

Do not try this at home.

teasing him, right into him. Patrick got really fired up and quickly scored twice because Scottie was under his skin.

He was trashin' him from the other side of the key saying, 'Luc's shutting you down' and Patrick's got a big frown on his face like 'F... you' and I was doing the same thing. I was like 'Shut the f... up, what are you talking about Scottie.' I've got to deal with him. Then Pip goes to the all-star break and apparently he was giving him some more about it. Then the next time we saw the Knicks, Patrick was loaded, ready to go. He didn't tear me up, but he certainly made a point of trying to. I think the closest he's come to tearing me up in quite a while was that one play-off game when he had so much success down the stretch.

New York has played a lot against us and knows the triangle offence nearly as well as we do. They match up well against us, they have the size and the power at most positions, but the reason they can't get over the hump, in all fairness, is they can't get over Michael. He is so dominant at his position and the rest of us aren't dominated, that he tips the balance. We have the skill players. I think Scottie and Michael are such skill players that we can handle the aggressive, physical style play of New York.

And they are very aggressive on the ball. And when they are that aggressive, the referees get used to it and kind of give them a break and let it go. So we had to adjust our game plan a little bit. You get used to playing that manner of basketball and they got one on us in New York just exactly through doing that. Sending two guys at the ball and over-extending the defence.

Michael was awesome

in the final 1:17 of regulation, scoring eight straight points, including a fall-away three that tied the scores at 88–88 with 19.4 seconds left. I'd shut Patrick down to two points in the fourth quarter of Game Two, but he nailed a clutch jumper with 38.9 seconds remaining in the overtime that gave them the lead for good and took Game Three 102–99. At 2–1, we didn't think they were a chance, but it was ridiculous to think we'd go through the play-offs undefeated. It was nice to finally get the monkey off our back in a way. Obviously we were upset with ourselves for not playing well, but again we came back from a big deficit and put it into overtime and we felt good about that.

We felt we had taken their best punch, after they had made all the adjustments from the first two games. And once you beat a team twice in a play-off series, it really is about coaching adjustments, which is one of the reasons we're successful, because Phil's the master at that aspect of hoops.

In New York, we couldn't make any more adjustments, everything we were doing was working. It's harder to make adjustments during the game than it is between them. So New York made the right adjustments and we couldn't figure it out until the last quarter by which time it was too late, we'd expended too much energy. That's why you see Michael scoring a lot in the fourth quarter. Sometimes it takes him three quarters, or against the not too good teams, only a half, to figure out where the double teams are coming from and what the defence is doing. He's figuring out their game plan if you will and once he's got it figured out—you're toast.

That's why we came back so well in Game Four, we made all the adjustments, which we do well on the fly. We had all the right areas of focus and took it from there. We kept Anthony Mason off the boards and out of the game basically, they had guys who had one good game and that's why we were confident all the way through the finals, we felt, to quote Steve Kerr:

'No-one would beat us four times.'

We felt in a seven-game series we had the advantage. It becomes a cerebral match-up too, which makes it interesting, you get to know a team so well, it becomes guessing, second guessing, and second guessing the second guess.

But sometimes you can sit back and watch. One of the fun things to watch in basketball is the Michael-John Starks match-up, because John was one of the first guards who really got up underneath Michael with nose-on-ball defence and aggressively had a go at him. There's a lot of residual aggression, so watch those two go at it. I've seen Michael pretty much dismantle guys when he decides to and it's fun to watch him struggle to do it, to have to fight to do it, to give it everything he's got. And Johnny Starks knows his game, he's got the book on Michael as much as anyone I suppose. He gives him trouble. It's fun to watch him get in there and give Michael a fair shake.

John Starks is a hard player to be a fan of and I'm not. He's one of those players that whenever he comes through the lane, I get a foul. He and Dikembe Mutombo are the two who are the hardest for me to keep from fouling. I take pleasure in it, but he's a slippery little bastard. He hit a shot on us where Patrick set an up screen from the baseline, I didn't get out quick enough and he beat me on the baseline, I reached in but he was by me, he went up at the ring, defenders were there, he spun, did a full 360 and flipped it back up on the front of the rim. It was an incredible shot and he's an incredible athlete.

New York is the wildest place of anywhere to be, especially for the

POSTING UP IN THE POST SEASON

Finals. Their fans are the craziest, the town is the craziest town I've been to on the planet. We stay in a very populous spot at the Plaza on Central Park and everyone knows where you're at, the entrances to that hotel become packed with fans, a lot of media, cameramen, TV crews from Chicago, New York. And this deep in the play-offs, there are less teams to cover so the media numbers are increasing, the density picks up. So they're fighting for stories and it's almost impossible to go outside and grab a taxi without doing four or five interviews.

I didn't have an alias at that point but halfway through the series I told reception not to let any calls through except if it was my wife. I was getting young men, college kids probably, calling me up and ripping me: 'Longley you suck!' or 'Patrick's going to kick your arse!' Basically they were abusing me, and we all got it. I guess it's their version of comedy, but it's not too good at one o'clock in the morning. So there's a lot of distractions in New York.

Madison Square Garden has an awesome atmosphere although it's a difficult arena to shoot in, we never jack it up well in New York, we always seem to shoot short, I don't know why. The fans are right there too. It's not like a lot of NBA arenas where the courtside fans are given binoculars upon entry, Knicks fans are right there beside the court, right behind the backboard and they're obnoxious.

And that front row opposite the bench attracts the Madonnas, Cindy Crawfords, Spike Lees and John McEnroes. Bill Murray's a big Bulls fans, but I think he lives in New York so he's at all our games which is good. I've got to meet Bill a few times and he's a fun guy to have at your games. It's kind of crazy to sit there on the bench and watch him, when he knows you're watching him and he's up to his tricks, putting on a bit of a show.

Nicole Kidman and Tom Cruise were there one time last season. It's a real event, the fans are loud, the building's got lots of history. Billy Baldwin came into the locker room after we won Game Four to hang out. We chatted for a while, but the boy had his New York jersey on and we all wanted to kick him out.

It's a blast to hit the streets and get abused, honked at by taxis. We've got our little breakfast nook, a little greasy spot that we go to on the corner in the morning. I'd love to live in New York for a year or two, I think it's a great place. It's got the best big man store in the world there too, Rochester Big and Tall. Well, the best branch of the best chain anyway, it's got everything. That side of New York makes playing in NY City serious fun. You feel like you're in the heart of it. New Yawk is my second favourite city to Chicago.

And MSG would be a great place to have as a home court, which is why it was doubly satisfying to take a win off them and leave up 3-1.

I don't think I've ever grinned harder when walking out of the Garden with a win. It's the hardest place in the world to grab a W. I've only done it three times I think. That night, up 3-1, the boys all broke out with cigars driving out of the arena, every one of us had a stogie in our hands and by the time we got to the plane, we were green. The bus was choked with smoke.

It looked like Cheech and Chong were out for a big night.

For some reason that was a big moment for us. Why we had the cigars out so early when we vowed not to do it during the Finals is a good question. For some reason we regard Madison Square Garden as a bogey ground, it's the devil's lair. We knew we had them at 3-1. The series was done as far as we were concerned and we were heading back to our place and our fans to put the semis to bed.

We wrapped up round two at home 94-81 and then headed out to Dennis's 35th birthday bash at the Crowbar. He had invited the whole city on the news the day before and the streets were closed down for three blocks around the club. When I arrived it was like game night—broadcast trucks, satellite dishes, fans going nuts, people wall to wall outside the bar. Just another night in Dennisville.

Eastern Conference final
vs Magic, 4-0

While we were taking care of business with the Knicks, the Magic was waiting patiently for us. And so we went from the most exciting city in America to the most boring—Orlando. It's just a dead town, they have Disneyworld there, but it's a town built around attractions and there's no attraction to the town, other than the attractions, which makes it a bit of a hole, if you know what I mean.

First we had two at home. We recognised Orlando was the team we had to go through if we were going to get anything done. The job I did on Shaq was going to be huge, but the Magic was also why we acquired Ron Harper, so we could get the big guard line-up. We played Ron, Scottie and Michael all year so we could match up with the big guards of Orlando. Penny Hardaway, Nick Anderson and Dennis Scott had hurt us in the past. They'd posted us up and we'd been too small.

For the coaching staff and Michael particularly, the loss to Orlando a year earlier had stuck in their craw. God, it stuck in all of our craws. The year before when they beat us in Chicago, the Magic guys had Horace on their shoulders and they were raising their hands to the crowd. This

Playing the Magic was what we were all about, all year.

year at Chicago the crowd was slowly calling out his name, baiting him with 'Horrrrace, Horrrrace, Horrrrace', when we beat them 4-0. The coaching staff was so well prepared for the Orlando series, I'd never seen anything like the notes, the breakdowns, the video that we viewed in preparation for Shaq Daddy and his boyz.

My job, while I'd been very important over the first two series, became crucial. And that was to play Shaq head-up as much as possible. We dug in a little bit from the wings, but it's hard to keep it legal in the NBA with the zone rules, especially when they space out on the wings so well for their shooters. So essentially, I had to guard O'Neal one-on-one. Finally I was going to wear him down and catch him in the pool.

All superstars in the NBA are given a little slack and that leniency can get them a long way, give them an inch and ... they'll dunk the shit out of it, usually on your head with plenty of trash to boot. The refs won't give Shaq the steps, like they afford Patrick, but Shaq is allowed to basically put his left shoulder on you and give you the bulldozer. I tried drawing the charge a couple of times early in the series and it resulted in serious facials (dunks). They gave him the benefit of the doubt. If you hit the deck for the charge the refs are thinking 'Ah you're flopping'.

Shaq is THE most powerful man I've ever come across.

LUC LONGLEY

He weighs about as much as a tractor, probably 320 pounds, and I weigh 280. But he's explosive. I don't know what his vertical leap is, but he's full of fast twitch muscle fibres and can get off the floor real quick, he's a brute. He looks strong and he's stronger than he looks, and he's developed a little jump hook in the middle of the lane and a turn-around jump shot, so you can't just play him for the drop-step dunk anymore. And you can't go with the 'HackaShaq routine' although the guy couldn't hit the side of a recording studio from the foul line. He might as well learn to dunk it from the 15 feet.

What really hurt us the year before was the whole 'three-headed monster' issue, where we had three centres who were going to use all those fouls to hack Shaq because he couldn't shoot free throws. He still can't. But that theory came back to bite us, because the refs had decided long ago they were going to blow the whistle, because we had 18 fouls to give. It was still the case with two centres and only 12 fouls. The refs were calling it tight.

You basically have to play Shaq with your sternum and you have to keep your arms up. Drop your arms to protect yourself and it's an automatic foul. Even with Patrick and Alonzo you can use a forearm and

You can see how Michael has redefined the game.

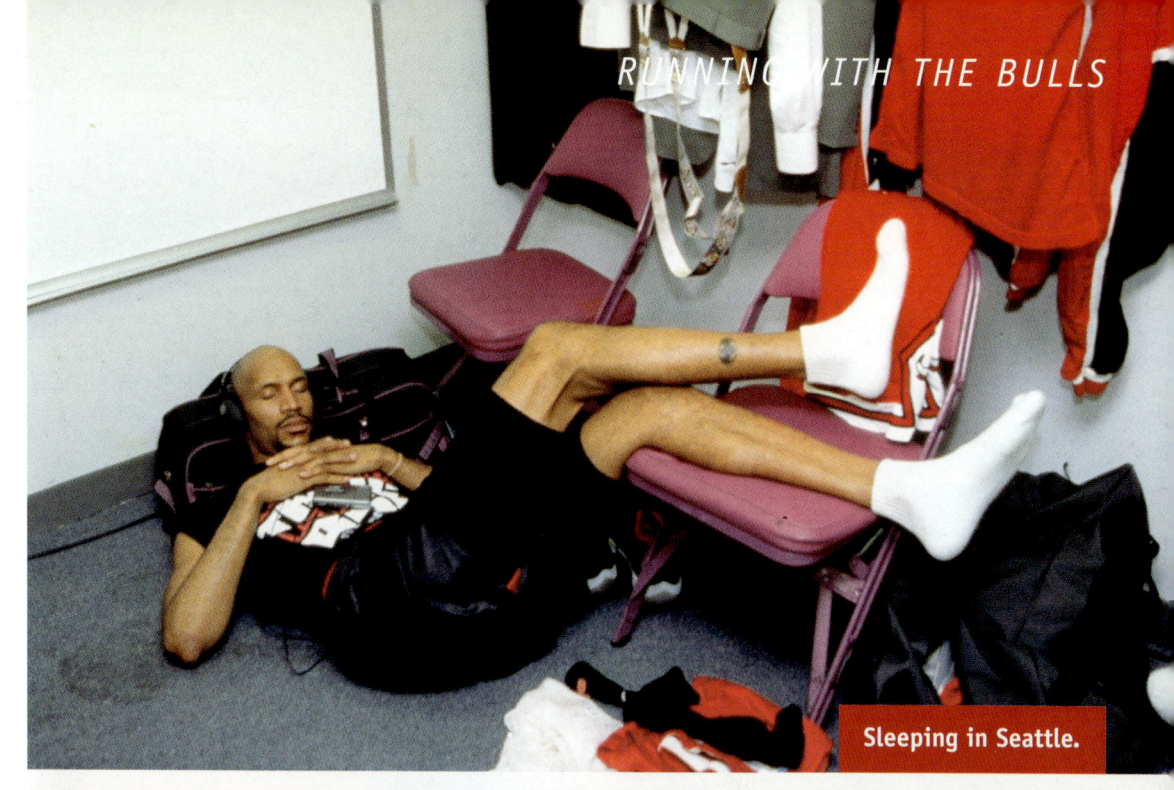

RUNNING WITH THE BULLS

Sleeping in Seattle.

Ron in the eye of a question tornado.

LUC LONGLEY

Post game in the locker room can be dazzling if you don't dress quickly enough.

Michael's view of the action.

RUNNING WITH THE BULLS

Thumbs up.

LUC LONGLEY

The coveted prize.

The spoils of an easy win.

wrist, but with Shaq I would do that, and because of his strength and momentum, he was able to break my forearm down almost at will. I wasn't getting anything done with my forearm, I was only using that to guide him in one direction a tad. I had to absorb all his force on my chest and believe me, that can start to hurt after a while.

It's like volunteering to be a crash test dummy.

Twice during that series, because I was absorbing all that force, I tweaked my back out. I've had that problem before in that he's so heavy, it's like being hit in the chest with a baseball bat. I missed one game against Boston in my first year with the Bulls after playing him. I just couldn't go, I was hurting. I got a back spasm from it. We have three masseuses on staff through the year and I think that really helped keeping everything loose and flexible. I had the odd manipulation from the chiropractor too. Dude, it's heavy work.

It's worth it. It's extra special beating Orlando because Shaq's the guy at my position who's the superstar, the Michael Jordan, the movie star, the rapper, the dollar spinner. It's nice to beat them. I didn't outplay him or outscore him or anything, but we did beat them and that's a feather in my cap really. It's something I'm very proud of.

He carries stardom around with him, he's bigger than life physically, but he has that demeanour about him, whether it's conjured or whether it's a form of charisma, I don't know. But he is the real thing. It was extra special to see them get swept and beat them in Orlando. And it's extra special to see him go out west so I don't have to see him quite so often. I must send the Lakers some chocolates. Maybe I'll be seeing Shaq again in the Finals with the Lakers.

The Magic had serious injury problems that series. Horace went out with a hyperextended left elbow in Game One and didn't return. Nick Anderson sprained his right wrist and missed Game Four, while Brian Shaw mysteriously suffered neck spasms and was out for the final two games of the sweep. Maybe he was lookin' for the broom. There were questions over their chemistry, they didn't look happy.

But we had no mercy, no sympathy and we weren't interested in this thing dragging on. 'We can't afford to feel sorry,' claimed Scottie. 'They didn't feel sorry for us last year when they beat us with Michael not having a full season.' We held the Magic to the second fewest points in play-off history on our 86-67 smoking in Game Three. Jordan had 45 in the final game, which we won 106-101. Mike said it was just a coincidence he had 45 points on the same floor on which he miscued a year earlier in the play-offs against the Magic. Yep, wearing No.45.

Had they beaten us, that franchise may have stayed together a bit longer. The fact that team is now dismantled is perhaps a legacy of our win. I'd like to think so, but maybe that's a bit ambitious. Perhaps Hollywood dismantled that team, who knows.

Shaq and I have spoken at times, but we don't hang, that's for sure. He was down in Australia a couple of years ago and said how much he liked it. There's also a lot of foul line banter while we're waiting for a free throw. Sometimes we're bagging the officials, sometimes we're talking shit to each other, getting the latest on nightclubs, the last play. 'That shit was unreal man', that sort of stuff. We got a lot of 'Take it easy on us tonight man' at the foul line this year. That was a first for me, or 'Be cool man'. And I'm like 'It's not me, you'd better talk to the guy on the foul line with the bald head. He's the one dismantling ya, I'm just a cog in the machine.'

We went through an amazing amount of cerebral preparation. We were super prepared. I've never been so focused. I was into the Miami and New York series, but then focused more than I ever have been for Orlando. As far as I was concerned, if we could get through these guys, Seattle or Utah wasn't going to be anything like this. This is what I could pin my pride on in the future, you know, to think 'We got through these three centres and finished with Shaq.' I was really into it.

The Orlando series was my big test.

I knew we'd come a long way through the course of the year, but I really considered them the most dangerous opponent. And we crushed them. My one-on-one defence on Shaq allowed us to clamp down on Anderson and Scott, who went a combined 2-of-17 on threes over the opening two games and missed 8-of-11 in Game Three. Dennis Rodman actually outscored Dennis Scott 46–29. It was the ultimate face job on Scott and the Magic.

What felt good about the Orlando sweep, is that it was the punctuation point. It justified all the hype. It gave us something to hang our hat on along with the 72 wins. ○

chapter 14

the big dance

**NBA Finals
vs Seattle, 4–2**

I think we had nine days off before the Finals and as I said, we're a very good team after we've had a chance to practice, but I think that was really pushing the envelope. Phil ran out of things to show us on video. We ended up having to scrimmage just to keep in game shape. It was a real challenge keeping that focus, that play-off edge. Play-off basketball is different in intensity, and it's a learning process. As you go deeper into the play-offs, you get better and better at it.

Phil really worked us hard that week but the time off also gave me a chance to take care of my knees. A lot of the guys put themselves in a play-off cocoon, they don't do anything except eat, sleep and think basketball in order for us to maintain that focus and form. When it's Spring, most of the other guys in the league are off in the Bahamas, the flowers are coming out ... when the flowers are coming out the season's over, when the leaves are on the trees, the season's coming to an end.

It's hot, muggy, the mosquitos are biting. It's not basketball weather, you want to go swimming, put some snags on the barbie, and sink some beers, all the things that come with summer. We had all this time on our hands and yet anything out of the ordinary felt like we were being untrue to ourselves. Consequently, the days were really long.

I wanted to go to bed early just to get the day over with like an eager kid waiting for Santa. The trouble was, we were playing our games at 7pm Chicago time, but in Seattle it would be 9pm Chicago time and games wouldn't finish until midnight. So I couldn't be going to sleep at 9pm during the week and then having to get up and play at 9pm in Seattle. The days were long and my kids were getting up at 6.30 because the sun was coming up. That was a long nine days and very frustrating.

Prior to the series opener,

Michael sent his teammates a subtle message without saying a thing.

We had a video meeting prior to Game One. The boys were ready to go to work, dressed in sweats and sneakers. MJ showed up in a sharp suit and tie, smoking a cigar. He had to go to a function, but nonetheless, he could have changed later. It was him saying 'Hey, this is the grand show, this is what I'm here for, this is what it's all about.' That was his statement about confidence, a statement that exuded arrogance really. It was nice to see MJ in that frame of mind, we had a battle to go fight.

We respected Seattle a great deal, primarily due to their defence, they dismantled us at their place. We had a 20-point lead, they withered it away and it was gone in the first 10 minutes, all with pressure defence. We had a reputation of being hot and cold against pressure defence—we'd either kill you, or fade. So it was good to get a chance to do a lot of work against that.

We had been so used to playing big centres but now my role in the big centre match-up was about to change. We were awkward about that. Bill was saying we should take a holiday, which was dangerous talk as well. I was thinking Ervin Johnson and Frank Brickowski—whom I think is a real good player. I wish we could have picked him up in free agency this summer—and Sam Perkins, who comes at you with a whole different look as a left-handed three-point shooter.

I never was really aware that Phil was going to play me on Shawn Kemp. When we got our Game One match-ups at practice, I thought 'Phil you bastard!', but in actual fact it was a relief because I'm so programmed to be defensively focused and that's how I generate my energy for the game. I work on defence and let my offence come to me. But I enjoy the responsibility of guarding the stud, and I especially enjoyed being the underdog in that match-up as I couldn't lose.

THE BIG DANCE

Kemp was a whole different challenge... real foot speed, real elevation, perimeter game. His game's not super refined, but he can blow by you and make you look silly very quickly. He's one of the supreme athletes in the league I reckon. I had to very quickly get some footage from our video crew and start doing some homework, but I wasn't alone in my study time. Kelly actually likes to watch videos with me and I probably watched at least a couple of hours of Shawn Kemp video the night I found out my assignment. I was fired up and looking forward to it.

As it happened he was their leading scorer and people say he played very well in the Finals and I agree, he did things in the Finals I hadn't seen out of him on the tape. He must have been saving some shit for the world audience. I gained a lot of respect for him and yet it wasn't to the extent a double team was forced that much. I still guarded him one-on-one and he didn't really kill us. I was pretty happy with the job I did on him.

Offensively I was able to use my size and get into it. I think Seattle's defence was so geared to Michael that once he put the ball

Challenging Kemp

on the floor, they were thinking 'Where are we coming from, who's trapping, where are our rotations?' They are a very organised defensive unit. Of our starters, Michael and Scottie are obvious offensive threats. Dennis is a consideration because of his work on the offensive glass, but

I'm like the fourth guy they worry about so they overlooked me.

They ran guys off me to double team the ball. They're not a strict defensive team in the sense that they stay at home and seal the lanes like a New York. They gamble, jump in the passing lanes, trap, scramble and recover all night. And in that scramble, I was able to find areas to the hole and the guys got me the ball.

Michael made a point of that at the start of the play-offs. He said, 'I'm going to be looking for you during this series, I reckon you'll be

121

LUC LONGLEY

Who said it's not a contact sport? Seven stitches.

open a lot.' In that first game he hit me a couple of times very early so that gave me a focus. I wound up scoring 14 points. But we struggled in the opener. The extended lay-off was showing. It took Toni to break out of a horrendous shooting slump where he was 3-of-36 from threes during the first three rounds, to put us over the top. He hit two threes, including a four-point play and we ran away with it 107–90. 'I was just waiting for one good game to come,' he said. 'I was beginning to wonder if I would be waiting until next year.'

In Game Two they changed what they were doing and I was out of it, just wasn't there. It was probably my worst game of the play-offs. I had more stitches in my eyebrow (seven) than points (two). That was courtesy of Kemp. It was a flailing elbow on a hard foul by somebody else. Dennis might have given him the old karate chop and I copped a whack. I tried to use that as motivation and the more I was angry and tried to be pissed off, the worse I played.

It was a lesson for me. People are always trying to get me to play that way, but my response is 'I know who I am, I know how I perform best. I'll stay that way thank you very much.' I think I let some of that stuff sink in. I saw it as a great opportunity to get really mad. It doesn't work with my make-up apparently. My head wasn't there, I wasn't focused or making good decisions. I did a good enough defensive job though and we went up 2-0 on a 92-88 win.

Dennis was incredible with 20 points and 21 rebounds, 11 at the offensive end, and he nailed a late free throw to seal the game. Sonics coach George Karl, who had ripped Dennis after Game One for his antics and con job on the NBA and their officials, particularly with Brickowski, said 'He was their MVP tonight.'

It was a thought provoking flight to the northwest for me. For Game Three in Seattle I was upset with myself after the Game Two shocker. I wanted to make a real emphasis of my offence and have a greater impact. The first two or three times I touched the ball I just drop stepped, put a shoulder into guys, looked at the rim and went for it. That hadn't been my role with the team, but in that situation, that night, it was fine.

I was focused. I had spoken to Michael a bit on the bus on the way to the game. He had told the media after Game Two he thought I was nervous, which is not true at all. I was feeling very comfortable with the whole play-off situation. I think I was over-aroused, partly because

THE BIG DANCE

of my eye and just over-confident in some respects. I think he understood after that discussion on the bus. That was the same discussion when I told him he couldn't go to Australia anymore because his profile had elevated since playing with me. I was just lightening it up on the bus before the game.

Of all the guys on the team, Steve Kerr's the best at looking for me and delivering me the ball, but Steve's not on all the time, so Scottie was the guy in that game. Of the starters, he's the guy that always tries to get me started and he got me going a couple times, and then Michael hit me a couple of times. My legs felt great that night which was weird, because I was battling some really sore knees. Maybe it was the salt in the air, the sea breeze ... who knows, but as I said earlier, I always play well in the shadow of the Space Needle, Seattle.

Defensively I was getting it done too. Shawn Kemp was having a horrible night. Everything I was doing against him was working, blocking his shots, you name it. It was a basketball highlight. I wasn't in the zone like in college where I had 35-point type games where I could hit anything, and things were happening for me. But I had a career play-off high 19 points nonetheless and with the help of some judicious double teams, held Shawn to 14 after he'd poured in 32 and 29 in Chicago.

In the first two games, because I'm not as quick as him, he was able to run the floor and get that good, deep post-up position in transition. In Game Three I concentrated on trying to beat him down the floor and wedge him out of that post position. And then we brought a double team to confuse him a little, to throw him off.

Things were happening for MJ too. He had 27 in the first half and we cruised 108–86. Phil said it was one of the best games we'd played all season and our best play-off game and he was right. A stunned Karl agreed. 'It was the first time I saw Chicago with the killer eyes in this series.'

After game three, I answered some questions that I had of myself and those of quite a lot of other people. I had that bad Game Two and inconsistency had often been a problem of mine, but to come out and have a good game, and be consistent through the remainder of the series, was nice to show myself I could bounce back from those sorts of disappointments. And it was great all that happened in front of global audience. That was something that was really satisfying.

Steve gave me a rap too. 'Luc in his career, may have had trouble getting focused at times,

he's kind of a laid back guy from Down Under.

LUC LONGLEY

'He's probably ridden harder than anybody on this team by Phil and Michael. And that's had an effect on him. He's become a much better player this year, a much tougher player. He withstands pressure a lot better than he used to.

'We had to have Luc in there, everybody knew that. He was the only one of the centres who had enough size to deal with guys like Shaq for an entire game. He was our one option and guys like that are not easy to find. There aren't many centres in the league that are as big and as strong, so he was our guy and everybody knew that. I think Dennis especially recognised that, because he more than anybody knows the value of defence and rebounding in the lane.'

Added Scottie: 'Seattle's a team that likes to junk up the defence, and

Feeding frenzy at the Finals.

if we can get some points inside, it really affects their defensive pressure. Luc's still in some ways the youngest player on the team and there's still a lot of learning to do. But he's a much better player than he was a year ago.'

Up 3-zip I told the media we had an exceptional group of leaders and it would stun me if we didn't come out very focused in the next game. I said 'We've managed to maintain incredible focus all year. That's one of the strengths of this team, that's why we've won all year and I don't think it's going to let us down in the fourth game of the Finals.'

Well, the cool, calm business-like Bulls got wrapped up in our own supremacy and we all fell victim to the SWEEP mentality. I was surprised at the extent it permeated the team. Even Michael had cigars on the bus ready to go. I had been down to the fish market in Seattle the day before and selected a whole Pacific King Salmon, it weighed about 35 pounds, and sent it back to my mother in Chicago. I thought 'We'll sweep, I'll be back in town tomorrow and we'll barbeque it and have a big celebration.' We were dominating Seattle, and had just swept Orlando. We were as cocky as hell.

I didn't know this, but Kelly smuggled a bottle of champagne into the game and hid it under her seat. All the karma was wrong and Phil felt it before the game. He said to me quietly before we walked out to the floor 'It's not good tonight Luc.' I didn't pay much attention, I was so into it, we were all high. But sure enough...

I'm a superstitious athlete,

as are many of the guys on the team and players in the NBA. Assistant coach Tex Winter's favourite saying is 'Things turn upon trifle', meaning the smallest things make the biggest difference. And our whole mindset really hurt us. Seattle came out with nothing to lose, super aggressive, just all over us defensively, like white on rice. Karl had told his troops 'Go back to playing crazy and out of control'. We couldn't move the ball, couldn't do anything off the dribble. Michael tried his best to save us, but couldn't get anything going. It wasn't meant for us that night and they blew us out 106–87.

They got some inspiration from Nate McMillan, but we missed Ronnie badly with a knee injury, it killed our rotations and weakened our guard defence. I think he'd been key all year. He did what I did—he did his job. He was our best guard post defender and Ron might be the best defender on the team, which doesn't fit his personality and profile after carving a reputation as a scoring highlight reel. But he's slowing down and he redesigned himself as a player and tailored it exactly to what the Bulls needed.

His role in our championship is not emphasised enough. He came up with big defensive plays right when we needed them. He and Toni were our X-factors, but Ron was more consistent and we won with defence. When it came down to the fourth quarter we stopped them, and talking to Dennis, John Salley and James Edwards, that was the same way they won championships at Detroit. When it came down to it, they could shut teams down and control possession. We made a point of it all year, and Ronnie was a big part of that.

LUC LONGLEY

Game Four was a shock. It was a reality check for all of us. It may be overstating it to say, but we might have got carried away with ourselves a little bit, the ease with which we'd won against Orlando 4–0, were up 3–0 on Seattle, even the way we finished off the Knicks. In many ways it was good that we lost so we had to go back and earn it again. It would have all been too easy had we swept them.

Seattle beat us and beat us well. We won the first three games and we didn't have any moves left to make. All the adjustments were in their favour. Yet what surprised me more than anything is that we didn't come back in Game Five and get it done, I was amazed they beat us twice in a row. Mind you, that's seen through the eyes of someone on a team who's just won nine games in a row and was feeling confident about itself.

We felt we had the ability to make the adjustments between games and felt the pressure was off us and was on them. We felt a lot better about it. We agreed that perhaps the cigars weren't a good idea or that Pearl Jam had been ready to play at the bar we were going to do. We went a bit overboard in our preparations and consequently focus waned.

Because before, after the Orlando series, we didn't have any hats, T-shirts or champagne. No celebration at all for the Eastern Conference championship. It was like another win, we walked into the locker room, showered and left. And I was really proud of that, because we had bigger fish to fry. That was cool and very classy on our part, then we let it slip in the Finals.

We did drop the ball on focus at the point. And the smallest things make a difference, as Tex says, and Seattle's defence had its tail up. They were all over the place like a mad dog's breakfast and Michael was having real trouble getting good looks. Scottie was struggling, Ron wasn't playing and he had been a game turner for us at times.

Ron can rise when he wants to and often did at crucial points in the game.

People seriously asked us 'Did you guys throw those games?' And tongue in cheek I told them 'Ah yeah man. Television ratings is what it's all about, people wanted to see Seattle get a couple of games, they wanted to see a series, and we get paid by the game, so we wanted a couple more. We really didn't find any good places to party in Seattle and the hotel was a bit crowd-

THE BIG DANCE

ed. A couple of us didn't tape, some didn't eat before the game, stuff like that ... so really we thought it was much better to win it back in Chicago.'

We couldn't pull out of the nose dive that quickly and that was a surprise to us. But again, in hindsight I'm glad it happened that way. I remember during the play-offs thinking 'I'm doing well, but could I do this well under a real pressure situation when we weren't rolling over people?' I'm glad it became more of a challenge, the games created more emotion, it became more important. You find about yourself a lot more than when you're up and in front and winning.

Stuck for solutions in Seattle after Game Five.

The Game Four victory inspired the Sonics a couple of days later and they got to within 3-2 on an 89-78 win in front of their deafening fans at Key Arena.

That was as close as they would get. I remember saying to Kelly that there was no way they would beat us in Chicago. I felt ultra confident. I didn't plan any parties, but I knew we'd get the job done. I could just tell, the demeanour of the guys on the plane on the way back was quieter and more intense. And we knew we'd been so good on our home court, losing just twice all year.

Nevertheless, we had a series going, but nothing gets Michael, Scottie, Dennis, me or any of the boys more into it than a challenge. We'd often beat teams by more if they played really hard and really well, because the guys got in to it. If teams lay down for us, we'd go to sleep, get disinterested. That's an indication of how good we were and I felt that would come out—and it did—when we got back to Chicago.

I've never felt the stadium so charged. We get big crowds for big games, but the stadium that night was absolutely buzzing. If you were a bit down on energy, you could generate energy from them no problem. Bulls fans like to chant Looooc, Looooc at home games and they did again this day. I kinda like that. When I'm playing bad, I can't really tell if they're booing me. The whole city was up and driving to the game, every car was decorated in the red and black of the Bulls.

It had a real AFL grand final atmosphere about it.

Everyone knew there was but one show in town. I don't have my windows tinted enough and it's a flash car, so people were looking in at me and Jud. We nearly caused traffic accidents. Once one person recognised us, people starting honking their horns, waving out of windows, wanting to talk to us. I was just hoping the traffic didn't stop, I thought we were going to get jumped.

In Game Six the Sonics had the momentum and the edge. It took us three quarters to grind them down and it took Michael three quarters to figure out how he was going to beat them. Never through that game, though, did I feel we were going to lose. I felt really positive about it, like it was meant to be, like any other home court game.

For the second time in the series, Dennis matched the Finals record for offensive rebounds in a game with 11. He continually came up with the loose ball, the big possession. Looking back, it was Dennis who put us over the top this year, despite Michael being back for a full season. I thought Dennis deserved the Finals MVP. He was a workhorse for us and without him, there's no doubt we wouldn't have won it all.

Michael obviously did a great job, but Dennis really did everything else. He put in an incredible rebounding effort and did everything that was hard. He took Kemp at times when I got in foul trouble or when we needed to change the look. He was the guy who had the energy all the way through, I thought he carried us with that energy. Dennis became only the fifth player in NBA history to win the rebounding title and then an NBA crown, following notable centres George Mikan, Bill Russell, Wilt Chamberlain and Moses Malone.

Late in Game Six there was a shot of me on television, sitting on the bench next to Bill with my head in my hands while everyone else was cheering. That was when Toni hit the second three in the fourth quarter and it appeared we'd nailed it, it was a done deal. That moment for me was a combination of ecstasy and agony.

Toni had had such a rough play-offs and we needed his scoring so much, we knew that when Toni comes to play, well we're almost unbeataBULL. Toni's been known as a clutch performer, someone to hit the big shot and win a game for you. He proved that again in Game Six.

Seattle's Detlef Schrempf acknowledged the impact Toni and I had on the series. He said, 'We gave them confidence early. We got Luc Longley going early and that makes everybody's job harder because we know Michael is going to see the ball every time down the court, and when other guys are confident, it makes things a lot tougher.'

I have a good friendship with Toni, I wanted him to play well so badly, as well as the fact it was certainly important for us. All those things combined to make it a powerful moment. At that point it was a powerful indicator to me, and I think a lot of the guys, that the whole team

World Champs!!

was there that day and we could start seeing the writing on the wall. For me there was a certain amount of disbelief, I was just begging for us to hang on. I wanted to get it done.

Kelly always talks to me about my need for delayed gratification. I don't enjoy something unless it takes a long time to get it. I have to wait all day to open my Christmas presents. I can't just open them all in the morning in a feeding frenzy, it's not the same. Delayed gratification for me is the best gratification. And that goes hand-in-hand with the fact that it was almost better Seattle won a couple of games—wait for it, wait for it, wait for it. Got it.

The journey is the reward. I was still having fun waiting for it. That was the most fun moment, when it was within our grasp but we still had to do that work. The last two or three minutes I knew we had it, but I wasn't prepared to cash in. I used this analogy during the playoffs in that I wasn't prepared to cash in on all our hard work until the end.

Once that whistle sounded for an 87–75 win and the championship, I expected I was going to want to cash in and go nuts. All the boys ran out to centre court and jumped on each other and I found myself hanging back, almost like a spectator, watching and absorbing. After a minute they came back out of the huddle and jumped on me. But I wanted to run in to the locker room and scream, release it all right there, in the sanctity of the back rooms.

The NBA wanted to have the celebration on the floor, but I would have preferred to go back to the locker. It took a while to work my way up on to the scorer's table. It was a powerful and private moment for me, performed in front of a world audience. That made it a little difficult. It wasn't until we went back to the inner sanctum of the locker room, before they opened it up to the masses, that I might have had my first scream.

It was interesting to observe myself in that situation not being able to cut sick, go wild right there on the spot. A couple of the other guys had similar reactions. Who? It's not for me to say.

After the title, Michael said, 'When I looked at my teammates and the lack of success a lot of these guys have had, that was part of my motivation to do whatever I could to be a leader of this team, to get to where a lot of them had dreams of getting. I'm just as happy for those guys, so they can go out of their careers as a champion.

'No matter what happens from this point, you can't take a championship away from Randy Brown, Jud Buechler, even Jack Haley, Luc Longley. All these guys who have bounced around from team to team and now they have finally got to a situation where they have played in the most ultimate dream of playing in the NBA, and that's for a championship and that's to win.'

We'd put so much into us, there was so much structure, focus and routine and suddenly having arrived at this goal, a sort of mythical thing all year, it was powerful and it froze me in a way. It was like being in a vacuum. Then I looked across at Kelly, mum, dad, dad's wife Kat, who were in the stands and getting into it and obviously pretty proud and that was cool too to have them there watching it all.

It was Father's Day, I had dad in the locker room and it was pretty special for him. Obviously it was special for Michael, it was Father's Day two years earlier when he won his last championship with the Bulls and of course his father, who was murdered a few months later, was there. My dad was swollen with pride. All the fathers went out to Seattle for the victory celebrations thinking it would all be over in four or maybe five games. Not as many made it back to Chicago.

Having dad and mum there made a big difference.

Dad was a big influence in terms of basketball inspiration and having him talking to the Australian press outside the locker, drenched in champagne and all excited, was good stuff. Mum was equally as proud and she's been here in Chicago and seen the progression from when I first got here. She knows how hard I've worked.

Needless to say the salmon I bought in Seattle was never eaten. It was hot, mum was with me out west for Game Five and the neighbourhood ate it before it went off. I think they froze a small portion for us. It was a small price to pay. ○

chapter 15

the ring is the thing, time to party

Mayhem, madness, merry. That would aptly describe the after-match festivities that unfolded after the title had so rightly been reclaimed by the Bulls. It was the first time the NBA had ever had the championship presentation ceremony on the court, so they wanted us out there for television. No problem. After all, it's the lucrative TV broadcast rights that help pay our salaries by way of increasing the salary cap in our collective bargaining agreement. We were on-court for 45 minutes to an hour accepting the plaudits from the fans and the league. We raised the trophy to the fans and they went nuts as expected. They had played such an important part in the whole journey. We owed them something for sure and they were delirious with joy.

Of the four titles, it was only the second to be won on the Bulls' home floor. It was special not just for us, but them too. The boys soon had the cigars out, championship hats and t-shirts.

We were like kids, running around, hugging each other.

It was especially significant for the guys who hadn't won a ring before, like me, Ronnie, Bill, Steve, Toni, Jud and the rest of the guys. There were photo sessions with owner Jerry Reinsdorf, general manager Jerry Krause, who was lauded as the man who put the team

LUC LONGLEY

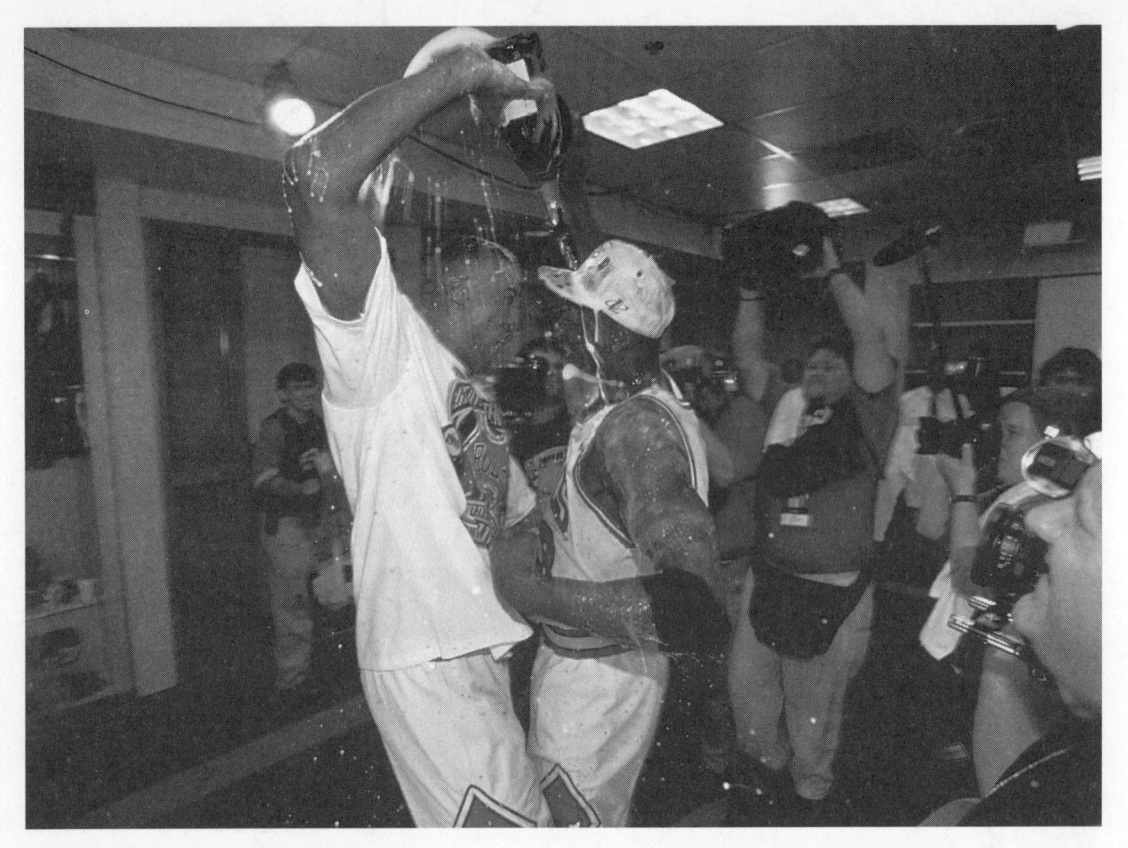

An athletic embrace.

together and of course Phil, who put it in to practice and got the job done with incredible preparation.

With the formalities out of the way, we waded our way through the pulling and tugging of hangers-on, back to the sanctity of the locker room and through to the very rear section, the weights room, that for any other game would be off-limits to everyone except Bulls staff and players. It was time for our own celebration.

It didn't take long for the champagne heavens to open up. Everyone was drenched, no-one was spared. Our individual lockers had been covered with plastic to protect our clothes. While we hadn't formally planned any post-game celebrations, one of the trainers was obviously ready.

When we came out to the locker room it was wall-to-wall with reporters. At this stage we were still in our uniforms soaked in bubbly, walking around in champagne-filled shoes. We still hadn't even cut our tape off. In the Bulls change room area, there is the locker room, training room and weights room, that's the order it goes in. Very quickly, the place was like a semi-trailer full of beef being trucked to an abattoir. Nowhere to run, and certainly nowhere to hide. Talk about loose and festive, the security guards were drinking champagne and having a ball. Every man and his dog got in, people I hadn't even seen before were there. I got a bunch of my friends in that my teammates had never seen before either.

Bill Wennington was primed. He had toiled pretty hard in the NBA and to finally win a championship was great for him. He's a good man and loves a beer and a good time. It didn't take him long to deduce that as long as he was wet, so too should everyone else. He was filling up tubs of water from the therapy pools and dousing everyone. Thousands of dollars worth of TV camera gear was copping it, but it made for great television. We were stuck in the weights room, pinned in basically. We couldn't leave the arena because all our gear was in the locker room. And we couldn't go into the locker room, because you couldn't get out there, there was so many media all trying to stick their camera in the door, it was peak hour.

We stuck our heads out and said g'day. If we had gone out there we would have spent the whole time doing interviews. We'd already done a ton. We were stuck in the locker room for two hours. I ended up hassling the security guards like 'Let's go, let's clear the locker room out so we can have a shower and get out of here.' It was almost three hours after the siren that I got in the shower. But I had Kelly, dad, his wife, and my mum back there and a mate from college, Rob Robbins, and a couple more friends who happened to be in town. I was happy to hang with them for a while, but we wanted to get out downtown.

Nothing was organised for the night of the championship and for a reason. The problem during the Finals is that we had made plans before and lost. We'd made plans in Seattle, so it was now an unwritten rule, don't buy any cigars, don't make any plans for a party, don't jinx ourselves. Win it and then worry about partying.

We had no idea where Michael was through all this. From the moment the siren went off, he was in his own world. I didn't even talk to him. He was wrapped up in his own emotions. One minute he was crying, the next he was smoking a cigar.

It was like he'd gone to the moon.

All the players had filtered out at different times because they were doing interviews. There was no planned deal for the above reasons. I think there was something upstairs in the boardroom, but you know, whoopee. The best thing as far as I was concerned was to hang with Dennis. He was ready to roll, pumped as usual, more so because he had a third title to his name, after two with Detroit. He said 'Let's go, we're goin' to the Crowbar.'

I told him 'Great, I'll see you there, I'm bringing my parents.' He loved that. You could just tell this was going to be special. If Dennis had anything to do with it, it would be worth remembering.

We jumped in the car, and were on our way to the Crowbar. By the time we got out of the United Center for the last time it was late, though the same fans who harangued me for game shoes after every home contest at the edge of the players' carpark were still there, and in party mode. They would have loved some championship paraphernalia. Not tonight boys.

The Crowbar is funky to say the least and very different, tucked away to the north of town near Cabrini Green, the badlands of Chicago. It was a warm June night, but the crowds were down at first glance, sort of quiet outside, no line-ups, which made for a hassle-free entry. The first thing we saw upon entry were guys in G-strings dancing in cages.

Championship night in Chicago was also Gay Night at the Crowbar.

Everyone inside was just as happy as anyone about the championship. They were fired up, partying and now we were there, the place was going mad. Typically, we beat Dennis there, who knows what got him delayed but we were escorted back in to a little corner that wrapped around the bar, almost our own little spot where we could view the whole place. The one constant, which was perhaps a tad overdone, was that we were surrounded by security guards the whole night.

Now, I didn't mind the protection, it allowed us to have some peace and enjoy the night, but when I got up to go the bathroom, a bouncer came with me. They were employed by the Crowbar, not the players. And it didn't really matter which bathroom I went too, I couldn't tell the difference by the end of the night. I certainly couldn't tell by the line-up. I didn't know who were men or women. But these guys walked us into the bathroom, took us to a stall and stood facing out, making sure no-one took a run at us while we were at the loo. I don't know what they were expecting. But I'm talking serious, full-on security, all packin' guns.

When my shadow and I made it back to the table, Eddie Vedder, the lead singer from Pearl Jam, had showed up with Dennis and of course his body guard, George, and a friend of his, Kelly. It was starting to hot up and Dennis's presence really turned the Crowbar in to a jumping joint. We had a bunch of people in our section, so it was pretty cool. And you know, most gay people are very cool anyway and that's why Dennis hangs out there, because he's not the freak, the unusual one or the standout.

THE RING IS THE THING, TIME TO PARTY

Post championship with accomplished celebrator Eddie Vedder of Pearl Jam.

I'm the straight guy, actually, like 'Who's the big stiff?' I'm unusual because I'm not as wild, but it's an environment where it's very easy to relax in because there's no aggravation. People are much more into their own thing. People who have decided to be gay usually don't have too many hang-ups about who they are if they've figured that much out about themselves. So it's usually a cool crowd and it was again that night.

Make a move and security was right there with you. Dad and Kat went for a dance and were enveloped by three security guards. They followed them out to the middle of a packed dance floor and made a triangle around them. My wife Kelly and Eddie Vedder were out there dancing and getting into it, but surprisingly, no shadows, no security. Eddie's real small, you don't notice him too much in a crowd. But he was fired up, he's real good mates with Dennis. He loves the Bulls and was buying us drinks all night. I don't remember buying a beverage all evening.

Before long Bill showed up and his mood had only enhanced. He was up on stage with his shirt off, grinding away. Steve Kerr and his wife arrived and people in the neighbourhood got word the Bulls were in the house and the place, not surprisingly, started to fill up quick. It was

LUC LONGLEY

The tangible evidence of a long, yet rewarding grind.

a blast and Bill couldn't help himself, he'd had a few beers and was on the bar, sunnies on, just getting down having a ball.

While a championship perhaps warranted the obligatory hangover from hell, it wasn't a write-off night. I had a few drinks, but I was too busy enjoying the sensation of shedding a whole year's anticipation, aggravation, work, the whole deal. I had post-championship euphoria, and will have until training camp I bet. I was just feeling great about life. It was like reaching a milestone you can never turn back from, climbing a plateau that you know can ever drop below.

Admittedly it was not one I dreamed of as a kid or the day the T-Wolves drafted me in the NBA. But it grew on me coming to the Bulls, and as I worked for it. I've always worked for basketball, I just didn't know I was working for an NBA championship all that time. Realising and justifying all that work, I was so high, I didn't want to mask it with too much alcohol.

I was just buzzing on the whole feeling.

As expected, Dennis was just out there the whole time, embracing the public basically, letting the masses have an ever so small, portioned piece. He likes to get out amongst the crowd, being touched, he's a physical guy, he likes contact. He goes to places that are packed because of it. But we got home at a reasonable hour, 4 or 5am. I guess that's reasonable for a championship night. I left Dennis somewhere in the mosh pit. Did he make it home that night? I haven't asked him. ○

chapter 16

injury timeout

I always knew I was going to cop my fair share of criticism after I withdrew from the Olympic team. Believe me, it wasn't an easy decision, but I had one thing in mind—future health.

I had no idea of, nor was I prepared mentally or physically, for the pounding my body was about to embark on in the NBA. Not until my second or third year in the league did I realise how tough it was to play a lot of minutes every single night. My body's aged 10 years in the last three, no question. We'll often play four games in five nights, then one in three nights then another four games in five nights. Nine games in two weeks is nothing unusual. Throw in the travel factor, eating at odd hours, time changes, clingy fans in hotel lobbies and it gets weary. And every night I'm playing flat out, against much bigger guys up and down the hardwood. People say it's a non-contact sport, but I'm here to tell you, it's heavy work and it's taken its toll on me over the years.

All my problems have been below the waist, lower extremity stuff. I've had several foot injuries, a stress fracture the year before last, knee problems. I weigh 280 pounds and all the torque goes through the ankles, feet and knees. And it's not as if I'd just started playing basketball when I hit the pros either. I've been playing hoops every day basically since I was 15 and before that in high school, probably three times a week at least. I went to the Australian Institute of Sport in Canberra as a 16-year-old, and that's full-on every night, then it was college in New Mexico which is even more intense.

Right away it was obvious to Craig Purdham, physio at the AIS and

LUC LONGLEY

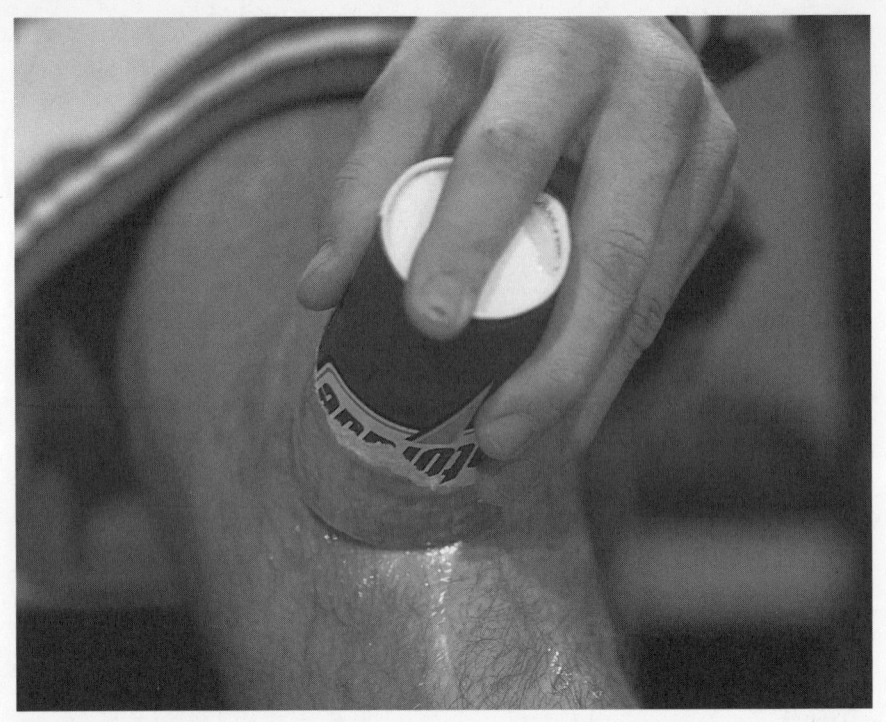

Ice is the price you pay.

our national team, and someone I put a lot of stock in, that I had bad flexibility in my ankles and it was giving me knee problems as a teenager. During my Institute days, I was projected to be 7'4", yet I was skeletally restricted, some bones were getting in the way and I wasn't growing right. And by playing every night, I developed bone spurs at the area of contact and as they grew, they made the ankles less and less flexible.

My ankles were like a fish tank, lots of debris floating around in a confined area. It got to a point this year that I had so little mobility in my ankle, it was sending all the shock up to my knee and back. I missed 20 games with knee problems. I tore a medial collateral ligament this year which needed two weeks' recovery.

For much of last season, I was working on a bum wheel. The Bulls medical staff, and Peter Harcourt, the Boomers' doctor, said

I was a ticking bomb waiting to explode.

I could feel it coming apart at the end of the season. I had cortisone injections in my right knee and I was favouring it so heavily because of my gammy left leg, the tendon was just a shambles.

The club was aware I was having problems of wear and tear and made some insurance moves early. They brought in veteran James Edwards as the second backup and then in March they brought in John Salley because I was having so many knee problems and my ankle was giving me so much buggery. Phil and the Bulls were concerned about it coming to a head before the end of the season. They honestly feared I wouldn't last the season.

I thought if I was to blow something out halfway through next season because I played the Olympics, I might sacrifice Sydney 2000 or I might sacrifice a couple of more years in the NBA. Surgery was something that had to happen right away to allow a full three-month summer to rehabilitate. Had I played the Olympics, I'd then have the surgery, but I'd be rehabbing during the season. And that can be dangerous because you want to get playing, you don't recover properly, you're not 100 per cent. To have the summer to rehabilitate and get strength levels back was crucial to me just for the longevity of my career.

I was motivated to have surgery immediately for another reason as well. What I don't want to get out of basketball is to become a cripple later in life. I lived with Bill Walton for three months one summer when I was in college, and the guy's a cripple, he couldn't play tennis with me, couldn't walk his dog. He played a little bit too long, pushed his body too far without taking care of it.

Kevin McHale too. I spent some time with him one summer when he was around at the Timberwolves after retiring from the Celtics, and he couldn't work with me, his body was gone, he couldn't even come out and show me things on the floor, it hurt him too much. Remember,

it takes something a little extra to lug a 7'2", 280 pound body up and down the floor 100 nights a year

and then bang against other guys of the same dimension. I don't want to be like Bill and Kevin. I want to be able to spend time with my kids. I don't think that is something you have to sacrifice.

Without doubt, the Bulls made it known they wanted me to have the surgery as soon as possible after the championship in preparation for next season. In many respects, I knew I was the number one centre on the team and wasn't going to give that up very easily. Not just the number one centre on the team, but the number one centre on the best team in the world. However, the Bulls could only exert so much pressure and I didn't really feel very much from them at all. I felt pressure from my ankle, knee and the way I had felt for the last half of the season. It was my decision. The Bulls would still love me and still want me back, whether I played the Olympics or not.

I spent four days at the Games watching the Boomers, but missed the great win over Croatia and the semi-final against the Dream Team, I was back in Chicago. But I had to return to Atlanta for the bronze medal play-off with Lithuania. I'm telling you, I was hurting not being part of it. And then seeing the way Arvydas Sabonis went to work on the team with 30 points and 13 rebounds, I'm not saying I would have made the difference, but another big body defensively certainly would not have gone astray. Regardless, I was proud of the boys for the way they played.

In some ways my decision to withdraw was the hard route,

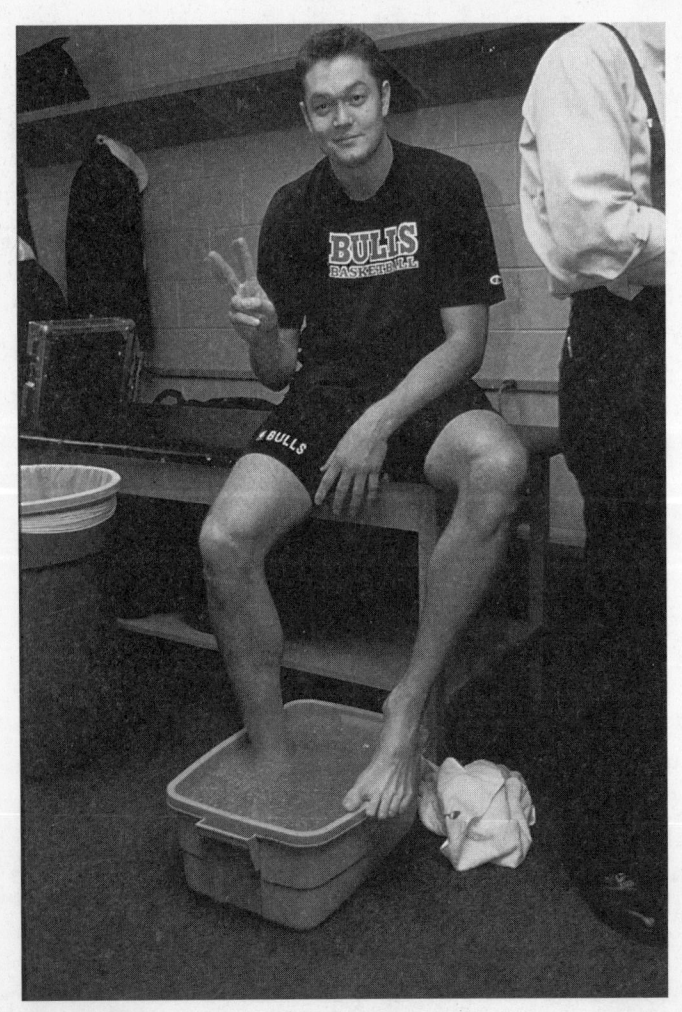

Freezing the pain.

the much harder option than to say no (to surgery) and do the right thing by everybody else. I always knew I would be criticised for it and people would think it was the soft option. I thought it was the hard option and being in Atlanta watching the team certainly brought it home to roost for me. I knew exactly how I was going to feel when I made the decision. I've played with those guys since I was young, Healy (Shane Heal), Andrew Vlahov, Hogie (Mark Bradtke). I've been playing with Andrew since under 12s.

I love the Olympics, they mean a lot to me. The Olympians were my idols as kids and being part of the national team at the Olympic Games is something that is still very important to me. It wasn't a decision I took lightly nor was it a decision made for any other reason than I didn't have any other choice in terms of my body. My

INJURY TIMEOUT

legs have always been a problem, I couldn't just blow it off for another year. I missed 18 games in a six week stretch late in the season and the Bulls pay me three million a year to play, not sit. I'm telling you, missing the Games was a crying shame, but I had some serious body

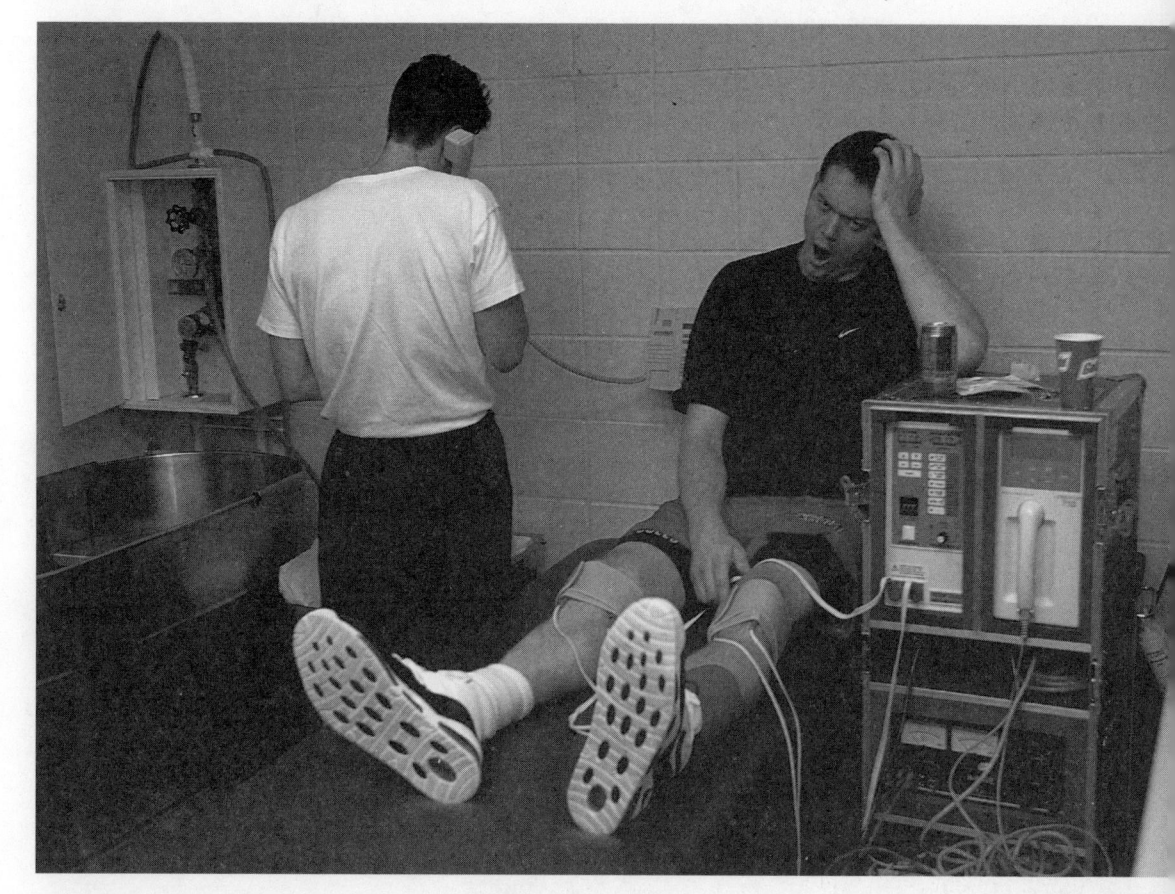

The longest hour of the day in post practice treatment.

maintenance to undergo.

It got to a point in the year where I had four ice bags on my knees, back and front, my ankle in an ice bucket, and an ice bag on my back. Getting out of bed the next morning was a symphony of cracks, pops and creaks. I was on a huge dose of anti-inflammatories. I was just managing the pain and inflammation and a world championship was what I did it for. We got that. I wasn't prepared to do that for, first, another couple of months, and second, I was not prepared to be crippled later on in life by pushing it too far and damaging something even further.

Who knows, I may have actually hurt the Boomers more than anything else. I was very cognisant of that, though it was a secondary consideration. I didn't want to fall between two stools; to go to the Olympics but not be able to perform as well as I'd like. With the Bulls I had a complementary role, but the Australian national team would have been totally different, and far more demanding. With the Boomers it meant I was going to have to take on a leadership role, a primary role. I just didn't think I was capable of that the way my body was feeling.

What hurts most is that it had the potential to be the greatest basketball year of all time for me, an NBA world championship and a medal at the Olympics. I knew exactly what I was giving up when I made the choice. Obviously, I felt like I was letting my teammates down and to a certain degree my country and basketball in Australia.

But playing would have meant giving up a lot personally too. All in the name of future health. ○

chapter 17

escaping the soul pirates

My summer haven is Australia, and more particularly my farm in southwest WA. I really prefer to call it a block. It started as a three-bedroom beach shack and we've added to it every year, done some renovations, cleared some paddocks. It's my hobby and the locals have rolled up their sleeves many times to give me a hand knocking it in to shape. It was my first purchase when I signed with the Timberwolves, something to do with that $1m signing bonus, although the block didn't cost that much.

It's incredibly serene. I have my own ocean frontage with killer waves. There are 200 metres of government land that no-one can own between me and the beach, but I'm the closest to the sand. The block has a fresh water spring that comes into a creek. I have about 350 acres, it's manageable and recently I employed a botanist for 12 months who lives there while I'm in Chicago, maintaining the gardens and surrounds.

The local town has a basketball court and some weight equipment. They had built a recreation centre and had some room but no gear, so I donated some weights, around 10 grands' worth I guess. In order for me to spend some time down there in summer, I had to be able to work out. So instead of buying a lot of really good gear and sticking it in a back room which I didn't have, I donated it to the local rec centre to give me a training base. In return for the weights I said I wanted a key, so I could go down any time of the day or night to lift or shoot around. It's got two courts, it's a nice place and they've been really good to me.

I find the farm a good place for my mental health, to get away from the soul pirates. In the Minnesota years I'd get there and try to regroup, rediscover the things that made me tick because I would get diluted in Minneapolis, worn down, worn away by all the losing. American culture is very different and sometimes it can be very abrasive on a guy's individuality.

I would get down to my farm and remember how to be an Australian again.

After my first stint with the Bulls, that would have been July 1994, I went down to the local town and was working out 5-6 mornings a week, doing sprints on the footy oval, running up sand hills in front of my joint and lifting weights. I even seconded a couple of the local lads to come with me, working as training partners. Some days, if it was a really nice morning we'd go fishing instead, it was pretty casual, but business-like too.

I could still work out and still be professional, but get my prescribed yearly dose of the bush, of Australia. Cities like Fremantle were getting more and more uncomfortable for me because people were getting to know me. I had to change the phone number this year. I put my name in the local phone book not thinking, I didn't realise it would be a problem five years ago when I bought the place. Five years later the media found out. They'd be calling at all hours and it became a pain. 'Did I have a comment on this, on that, the kid who killed himself hanging on the ring in Melbourne', calls right out of the blue.

Then they were door-stopping me. I had one guy from an unnamed television station at the main gate, but I wasn't there. Buffy, the girl who works on my property, met him at the gate which is 300-400m from the house, and he's got his cameraman and anchorwoman and it's like 'Where's Luc?' Buffy said 'Luc who?' He went on a spiel of how he knew I was there, knew the guy I bought the property from and so on.

Kelly was just pulling up and gets out of the car and said: 'I'm Mrs Longley, Luc isn't here, he's on holiday. He's done a media conference in Perth, he doesn't want to be hassled, this is his two weeks of solitude.'

Kelly got back in the car thinking she'd basically said 'Go away', drove to the main road which is over a hill, and the guy never comes. He's gone on down the track looking for me, wanting to get a shot of me on the tractor or something. I don't even own a tractor. So Kelly waits about two minutes and found him up at the house with his camera ready to go. I was really upset about it and I called the TV station and said 'Look, I've done interviews, I'm happy to do interviews, I've done a press conference in Perth, but please respect my privacy while I'm on my own property.'

But they found me. I've been down to the farm 4-5 months at a time in the past and never had a problem. Now I'm a Bull, things have changed. In the past people in Australia didn't understand the NBA or what was going on, they just thought I wasn't really living up to expectations. As soon as this championship happened with the Bulls, suddenly people's attitudes changed. Now they're going out of their way to help me, thank me, congratulate me or whatever. I'm flattered really, but it's difficult at times. Imagine what MJ feels every day of his life? ○

postscript

by Chris Appleby

*I*t was 9am Illinois time on a Thursday and the summer sun was beaming down on Riverwoods, a fashionable northern suburb of Chicago, where Luc resides. Already worn out from three days of shooting around on the Bulls' practice floor and throwing medicine balls at a wall, I warily ask Luc if we are going to work out today.

'Yeah,' he retorted, glaring down at me as his massive frame filled the doorway to the kitchen. 'It's my job!' He was almost disgusted I would even contemplate the thought of slacking off. It was late July and the start of the NBA season was still months away, but this is where his quest for a second championship started for Luc.

Three hours later, as we pound away at 60 metre sprints on the narrow strip of grass outside the club's Deerfield practice facility, I am either going to pass out or simply elect to die. It is at that stage I consider not even a $3m salary is worth all this muscle agony and oxygen deprivation.

But for Longley, it's all in a day's work. And it's been serious work since the humbling days when we played as teammates running the hardwood for the Ginninderra Rats in the ACT first division almost 12 years earlier.

No-one pushes Luc harder than Longley himself and all the trimmings that come with the NBA lifestyle mean little in a pair of training shoes or with 100 kilos across his shoulders. He drags himself out of bed and on to the weights room floor as quickly as he did back at the Australian Institute of Sport when the timely note that read 'Remember Why? 1988' hung above his doorway.

That script was the motivation for his claims to a berth at the Seoul Olympics which he duly achieved. Little did he know there were bigger fish to fry. Longley's accomplishments in the NBA no doubt fill the hearts of thousands of young Australian hoopers with endless motivation and drive. It is that very characteristic, although one that is not immediately noticeable about the likeable big fella, that has come to the fore and figured so prominently in recent years.

Many times Longley could have taken the easy route and turned his back on NBA life and financial security. Yet he persevered and along

POSTSCRIPT

the way conquered many challenges thrown at him. He didn't grow up in a US culture that bred basketball junkies, or play on asphalt playgrounds where the warriors of the NBA today once plied their craft. He did it the hard way, travelling from afar to crack it in the bigs and succeed.

Not only succeed, but prove anyone can make a difference if they put their mind to it. When battling through the low times at Minnesota in his rookie year, Luc predicted his NBA life would mirror his college days in terms of improvement, production and expectation. He said it would take four years. He was right on the money.

Australian basketball fans have had little access to Luc's story or the immense journey he has endured. From a nothing teenager more intent on taking things easy than taking a hard foul, Longley has blazed a pioneering trail for other Aussies to follow.

Now Olympic teammate and Sydney Kings guard Shane Heal will join him, ironically, with the T-Wolves, where it all started for Longley. Others may be on the way. Melbourne's Mark Bradtke is expected at the Philadelphia 76ers and a couple of Magic youngsters in seven footer Chris Anstey and the athletic Sam MacKinnon come to mind, so too Paul Rogers, an Adelaide native, now at Gonzaga University.

In many ways their shot at the big time has been made a tad easier because of Longley, who broke down the barriers and proved Australian talent was available and they could play—in any league.

At his final post-game press conference following the Game Six victory and championship, Longley talked about the experience of winning the most prized trophy in the NBA.

'I'm proud of it. I hope the people in Australia are getting some of this footage and can see how much fun we're having because it's a first, and hopefully not the last. It's great, you can't describe it.

'It's fulfilling and rewarding for all the work we've done. I think I might have worked harder this year than ever before in my career. That's sort of the way this whole team functions. This is the reward. Let's do it again.'

The Journey is the Reward. Now Luc's ready to tackle that journey one more time in a bid for back-to-back titles. ○